Vignettes:
A Short History of My Life
Including
"A Day in the Life of the Post Engineer"

John V. Richardson Sr.

SECOND EDITION

Los Angeles, California:
Information Transfer Associates Press

2013

Cataloging-in-Publication Data

Richardson, John V., 1918-2009.
  Vignettes: A Short History of My Life.

  Includes appendices.

1. Ohio--Autobiography.
2. World War, 1939-1945 -- Personal narratives, American.
3. Mining machinery industry -- Ohio -- Columbus.
4. Jeffrey Manufacturing Company (Columbus, Ohio).

920.092 R53

Requests for permission to make copies of any part of the work should be mailed to the following address: Permissions Department, ITA Press, 242 North Hillcrest Blvd., Inglewood, CA 90301-1354.

International Standard Book Number: 098191960X; 978-0-9819196-0-7

Library of Congress Control Number: pending

Printed in the United States of America

13 14 15 16 JR 9 8 7 6

Table of Contents

List of Illustrations

John V. Richardson

I was Born

I, John Vinson Richardson, was born July 24, 1918 in a hospital in Newark, Ohio.[1] My father worked for the Baltimore and Ohio Railroad as a bridge carpenter.[2] My mother was the keeper of the house. Prior to this time, my parents had held several positions: my Father as fireman on the Pennsylvania Railroad, tenant farmer, and farmer manager at the Orient State Farm Institution while my Mother managed the laundry at Orient, Ohio.[3]

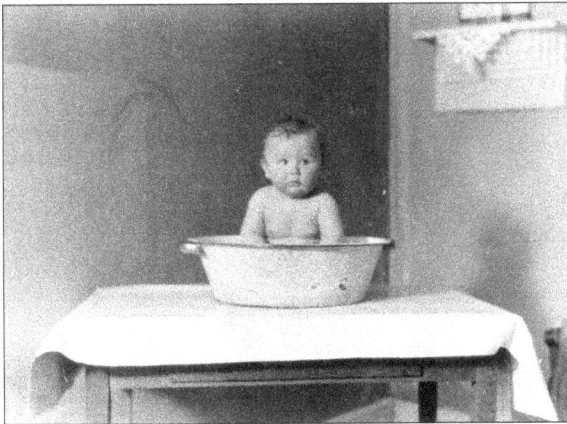

Figure 1. At Twelve Months, 1919

---

[1] I survived the 1918 Spanish influenza epidemic due to my mother's round-the-clock care; see Kirsty E. Duncan, *Hunting the 1918 Flu; One Scientist's Search for a Killer Virus* (Toronto: University of Toronto, 2003).

[2] See Sir Herman Richardson's union badges for the Brotherhood of Maintenance of Way, 1919 B&O Convention delegate ribbon, and photograph of Detroit September 1919 meeting and delegate badge with ribbon, which have been donated to the Newark Historical Society.

[3] For the Feeble-Minded. On the back of the pictured postcard, Bessie wrote: "This is the Cottage where we stay. The room marked with a cross is our room. Look close and you can see the iron bars on our windows and doors. I can't help it but I always did think I would land behind the bars."

Vignettes

The first story I recall my parents telling me: the day they were married it was the hottest day on record (September 22, 1910).[4] Shortly after their marriage, they went to a public sale/auction where they purchased a Waterbury 24-hour clock--the purchase price, twenty-five cents.[5] Dad also purchased a shotgun. It was a 12-gauge, 30-inch barrel, full choke.[6] They started married life in Bloom Township, Morgan County (Ohio), near Rural Dale. Dad was a farm hand for Bob Miller who owned several hundred acres in Bloom Township. There was a tenant house on the land and this site is where they went to set up housekeeping. They had a few chickens and a horse or two. They grew most of the food they needed, except for flour and coffee.[7] One day in winter, Dad took a basket of eggs and started to ride

---

[4] The state record of 113 degrees was set in 1934 near Gallipolis, Ohio.

[5] According to the "Ledger" of Bessie Richardson, my mother, the clock was "purchased by [Harriett and John] Humphreys at farm auction in 1920 for 25 cents. She inherited it from Harriett Hughes Humphrey estate in 1960s. Restored and refinished at that time. Appraised in the 1970s at $175." In any event, this clock, with its paper label and a red "1105" label, stood for forty years on the grandmother desk at 614 East Schreyer Place, Columbus Ohio.

[6] This gun hung over the wood burning stove at DaySpring Farm in Morgan County, Ohio until it was stolen on Memorial Day Weekend 1999.

[7] At Thanksgiving 2007, Hope and I reflected on my mother's rhubarb and grape pies: "She did make a raisin pie, as well, and I remember mincemeat. When I [Hope] started making the Concord Grape Pie, I looked in a cookbook for a recipe and discovered how to get rid of the seeds; his mother just always used whole grapes, but I did the pie without the seed. John was so pleased that he wanted me to share my recipe, but I wouldn't, I didn't want to hurt her feelings. She made pumpkin pies for Thanksgiving, along with the mincemeat. He also remembers that she'd bake a cherry pie for Washington's Birthday and a Lincoln's Log for Lincoln's birthday. Maybe that is where I got the idea. In July, John would go across the road and pick blackberries for pies. His mother's real forte was angel food cake; she made one as our wedding cake. She had a wide reputation for those cakes and John says that her secret was adding an extra egg white (recipe only calls for a dozen). We have tried to remember other cooking that she did. You probably remember Christmases. For supper on Christmas, we always were at her house (dinner was at noon, at the Smiths). She would fry oysters – I still remember those and I never did them as well as she did. Probably she fried them in lard after dipping them in cornmeal. You will remember that she always made a hot dog for you because you did not like oysters. John has tried to remember other things that she prepared. They always made horseradish in early spring, as soon as the leaves came up and they could find the row of plants (see appendix 3 for a recipe). John did not like the condiment so well, but they made it as gift to Uncle Ed Humphrey, Namo's brother, who lived in Malta. In September, when squirrel hunting was in season, Sir Herman would shoot a squirrel. She would boil the skinned pieces until tender, then coat them with flour and brown them in a skillet, making gravy. She also would do rabbit in much the same way, but Dad did not care about that. She did cook quail a few times, but he can't really remember excepting it tasted like a mild chicken. There were quail around even after we got the farm, but we had a deep snow in January one year that stayed on the ground and hungry foxes got all of the quail. There have been none since. While on the subject of food, Sir Herman would bring in ears of field corn after the ears had matured but before the cutting began, and grate the grain on a box grater and

horse back to a little store at Rural Dale, which was four miles away. Roads were muddy. The horse tripped in the mud throwing Dad and his eggs off the horse. Dad was not hurt, but the eggs were scrambled. Needless to say, they had no coffee, sugar, or flour until the hens laid some more eggs. They lived in a barter economy.

---

cook it into mush. We would call it polenta today."

Vignettes

Squirrel Hunting

The shotgun that my father purchased at the auction served him well. It was used to hunt squirrel and rabbits. When the squirrel law came in during September of each year, the shotgun provided us with fresh meat. During the summer, it kept the groundhogs from getting into the springhouse. My father taught me the proper use of the shotgun as well as the twenty-two pump rifle he had acquired. Finally one day he said, "John, you are old enough to squirrel hunt by yourself." As I picked up the gun, he said, "Now don't point it straight up at a squirrel." Apparently, I forgot his warning. The squirrel was in the top of a tall butternut tree, across the road and in a deep hollow. I was standing in the creek bed, trying to get a good sight on the squirrel. I fired the shot and the gun went off. As I picked myself up out of the creek bed, I realized I had a real gusher of a nosebleed and my cheek felt strange. I got back to the house without the squirrel—couldn't find it. Dad looked at me and said, "You didn't listen to me, did you?" He didn't scold me; he didn't need to.

John V. Richardson

The 1913 Muskingum Flood[8]

If I recollect correctly, my parents moved from the Bob Miller farm to the Mart Anderson farm on the Muskingum River.[9] Again, Dad was the farm hand and Mom kept house and did the gardening. According to a story they told me, there were torrential rains in March 1913. The Muskingum River was way above what was considered flood stage. This event occurred before the government's flood control projects. My parents had left the farmhouse to wait out the flood. For some reason, my father thought it necessary to go back to the house even though the first floor was under water. He got in a Jon boat. All farms along the river had these boats for fishing. He rowed to the house and went in the window on the second floor, picked up whatever it was he had gone after. He got back into the Jon boat and headed for shore, when a large tree hit the boat and smashed it. Dad grabbed the limb of a pear tree and hung on. The river was muddy—dead horses, cows, dogs, chicken, and sheep were floating past. Houses, buildings, lumber, trees were all floating down. Mom on the shore and Dad in the pear tree--each started calling for help! Help came from a person (or persons as you'll see later) on the other side of the river. A farmer by the name of Sile McClehiny rowed across the river through all the debris and swift current, picked Dad up, deposited him on shore with my mother and then rowed back across the river.

During July 1995, I spoke with a descendent of Sile's. Her story is that Sile took his two sons with him on this rescue mission. She also told me Sile liked his liquor. Dad had suggested that maybe Sile had had a few snorts too many but Dad was always thankful that Sile crossed the river and got him out of the pear tree. So am I. Furniture in the house was ruined, so relatives and neighbors pitched in and gave them the second start on housekeeping.[10]

---

[8] Due solely to excessive rainfall in the Muskingum's headwaters, the flood lasted from 23 March to 8 April 1913. According to the Marietta Times, it was the largest flood in the state's history and wiped out the canal and eleven locks; most of the towns along the river went into an economic decline from which they never recovered, according to their July 2000 website (accessed 21 December 2002).

[9] The creation of Rockeby Lock Number 8 in 1836 made this area attractive along with the availability of salt.

[10] The dining room table, sold at DaySpring Farm in 2006, is the lone survivor of that flood.

Vignettes

The Feeble-Minded Institute

Following this escapade, my parents worked at the "Feeble Minded Institute" in Orient, Ohio west of Columbus. Dad was farm boss and Mother managed the laundry. How long they were there is not clear in my recollection of stories told. Following this, they held similar jobs at the "Children's Home" at Avondale, just outside of Zanesville [on Ohio maps, it appears rather further east of Zanesville].

Figure 2. Cottage at the State Farm Institution at Orient, Ohio

John V. Richardson

Then to Railroad Jobs

They first lived in Columbus, Ohio. Dad fired the steam engines that ran between Columbus and Toledo. All that these trains pulled were coal cars and wartime material. How long this job lasted I don't recall. Next, he was working as a bridge carpenter for the Baltimore & Ohio Railroad and living in Newark, Ohio.[11] Dad got involved with a union organization U. B. M. W. E. R. S. L.[12] and in September 1919, he went to a big union-organizing meeting in Detroit.[13] He was very active as I recollect my mother's comments.[14]

Then they moved from Columbus to Newark (how they got their belongings there, I don't know). But, they hired a man and his wagon to move them three different times in one week. The mover finally said to them, "I hope you get to where you are going." They finally rented a house at 48 Gay Street in Newark. Then I was born July 24, 1918 in a hospital there.[15]

---

[11] My father, S. Herman, carried an Elgin Nat'l Watch Co. (U.S.A.) 15S, 7J OF sidewinder Model 2—4 (lever set) with Montgomery style Railroad dial (Serial No. 13610531, circa 1908) in a Keystone Silveroid case (Serial No. 8166262 with matching serial number bezel) with nine marks, other writing, and outside shield for engraved initials; in fair condition today.

[12] The "Brotherhood of Maintenance of Way;" see http://www.bmwe.org/ (accessed 13 April 2009).

[13] See the 10" x 36" union photograph in the Newark Historical Society; Herman is in top row, right hand side.

[14] Dad was a Republican and Mom was a Democrat.

[15] Being born in a hospital made me different [as] I found out from my first and second grade classmates. We were talking about where we were born—they were all born at home, most in the same house they were living in. I was pointed out as different.

Vignettes

Growing Up/School Days

I have no recollection of Newark at all. My earliest recollection is of living in a house on Oil Spring Run called the "Pickerel House" near Malta, Ohio. My parents moved there in 1921, probably in March. Dad rented the farm, raised corn, wheat, and hay. Mom ran the house, raised a garden, and tried to keep me out of the creek. The house had a picket fence around it, but I soon managed the latch on the gate. Crayfish, salamanders, and water bugs soon became friends.

I had another friend. No one could see him or talk to him except me. His name was Jay Haw. We played together out in the yard and in the house. There were no neighbors nearby and I barely knew some of my cousins, so I "invented" a friend. Where the name came from, I am only guessing. My father cultivated the garden with a horse and a single shovel cultivator or maybe a five shovel cultivator to keep the weeds down between the rows of corn, cabbage, potatoes, etc. If he wanted the horse to bear to the right, he would call out "Gee." If he wanted the horse to bear to the left, he would call out "Haw." So, I may have translated this command into Jay Haw. I loved to play out in the yard after dinner. We called it supper then. One evening, just at dark, a whippoorwill landed on the path, just outside the garden gate and started to sing. He really scared me! I cried and cried. For years after that I was afraid of the dark. I didn't want to go to bed or go from room to room if it was dark.

Out behind the barn was an oil well. The well was very shallow. At high noon, you could look down into the well, which was cased with two-inch planks— not the modern day steel pipe. You could see the gas bubbling through the oil. Dad would tie a tin can to a piece of binder twine and dip oil out to lubricate the farm machinery. The well is long gone, but oil still seeps from the rocks along the side of the hill. Hence, the name "Oil Spring Road." The house is long gone but several of the original foundation stones (twelve inches by thirteen inches by five feet, each weighing 900 pounds) frame the herb garden on the south end of the house at DaySpring.[16]

One Saturday afternoon, Dad washed the buggy in preparation for going to church about three quarters of a mile away.[17] Sunday morning came and Dad had

---

[16] The farm called DaySpring is featured in Carol Creuss Pflumm's *Hearthstrings: How To Make Decorative Garlands for All Seasons* (New York: Viking Studio Books, 1993), p. 49.

the horse harnessed and hitched to the buggy. Mom had chased me down finally and got the middy blouse over my head. I was afraid I would smother when she pulled it over my head. I was hard to catch! Finally dressed, we climbed into the buggy, late. This horse was retired from the Zanesville fire department. He had three speeds: walk, trot (maybe), and then overdrive. The key to driving this horse was the flick of the lines. Flick once—and you got a walk; flick twice and you got a trot, maybe; flick three times and you were in overdrive. Dad went straight to three flicks and we were off. Trees and bushes flying by. Dust flying. That horse was born to run. Good thing no one else was on the road; we wheeled into the churchyard and slid to a halt. Dad tied the horse to a tree and all the horses nickered good morning to each other. As I looked around, I saw a horse with a sidesaddle. Its rider would be Aunt Jenny Humphrey, my mother's sister in law. She was very proper. Nearby a wagon pulled by a team of bay horses was tied to another tree. The wagon bed was filled with straw and a couple of chairs as well as the wagon seat—this belonged to the Boles' family. They had a passel of kids.

We went into the building, Dad through the left door, Mom and I through the right hand side. In those days and at this congregation, men sat on the left side pews and the women on the right. There was a center aisle. Preacher Niehizer did it all, song leading, sermon, and preaching. I sat there with my legs dangling over the seat, hardly breathing. The preacher was talking about brotherly love and if you were baptized[18] you would have a home in heaven and brothers all over the world. This sermon was heavy going for a four to five year old. I whispered to Mom that I didn't have any brothers to love me. She shushed me and I stayed shushed until we got home. Mom tried to explain why I didn't have a brother or sister, but that went over my head. In the mid-1980s, I did meet a brother from India[19] so Preacher Niehizer's sermon came true.

While we lived at the Pickerel Place, it was necessary to go to Malta/McConnelsville for grocery, seeds, and so on--all those things necessary to operate a farm. My mother's parents lived between the Pickerel Place and Malta. They dropped me off with Grandma. She always gave me a dime when we left, that

---

[17] The United Brethren in Christ in Oil Springs Charge is near Triadelphia, a stop along the Underground Railroad in the early 19th century; see also James J. Weaver's "A Burying Ground," *Columbus Dispatch Magazine*, 22 July 1979, p. 41.

[18] Not until much later as Lieutenant John Richardson, Baptismal Certificate, 2 January 1944 at the Seventh and Camp Streets Church of Christ in New Orleans, Louisiana, signed by Frank M. Mullins, Minister.

[19] The congregation where we attended (i.e., Indian Springs Church of Christ) was supporting a preacher from India and he was in Columbus to make a report; his name was RajRal.

would buy a package of chewing gum with a nickel left over for my piggy bank, a little red barn with a slot in the roof. Grandfather Humphrey was a farmer, hunter, trapper, wine maker, and storyteller.[20]

Figure 3. John Humphrey, JVR, and Charles Maris

I enjoyed sitting on Grandfather's lap. He wore a sheepskin coat in the wintertime. I would snuggle up in the coat with him and felt loved. After awhile, Grandfather got tired of my squirming around and he would light his pipe. He smoked Five Brothers tobacco.[21] It was the strongest on the market. He would blow a puff of smoke into the coat and I was gone. He had a good friend, Cyrus Bankes, who was Albert Bankes' uncle (Albert is Hope's grandfather). They both loved to hunt fox and raccoon. I enjoyed the stories they told about their hunts and especially Shawnee Indian stories. Cyrus was the local telephone fixer upper. Telephone lines were one strand of wire on insulators, sometimes on poles, and many times, the insulators were nailed to a tree.

---

[20] He owned an Elgin Nat'l Watch Company (12S, 5?J OF Model 23, though no lever to set it) with a Montgomery style Railroad dial (Serial No. 214749343 (circa 1918) in a Philadelphia Watch Company Silverode Case (Serial No. 716237 with matching serial number bezel) with dates marked. When I inherited it, the bow rocked, and it was in fair condition. I also owned a red and black wooden "O-Boy Duncan Yo-Yo," but my real joy was Go-Go, a yellow riding toy, made by his son, Ed Humphrey who was a carpenter.

[21] "One of the more unusual tobaccos available, extremely full-bodied, ultra-high nicotene (sic) content" according to http://www.tobaccoreviews.com/blend_detail.cfm?ALPHA=F&TID=1138 (accessed 30 October 2007). He may have been supplied by his daughter, Clarissa, who worked in the local tobacco factory.

John V. Richardson

Vignettes

About the Wine

Grandfather Humphrey made dandelion, cherry, blackberry, grape, and apple cider; whatever kind of fruit he had, he could turn into wine. Every lunch time, he would go into the cellar and do a little testing. He had a tin cup and he would have a taste of this and a taste of that. He would let me put my lips to the cup but I don't believe that I ever really tasted it—I think he let me pretend. The wines were in small three, five, and ten gallon wooden barrels and a whole row of them. Grandmother always threw a tizzy at Grandfather for taking me on his wine tasting journeys to the cellar. Sometimes I was allowed to stay overnight with Grandparents Humphrey. That was always a treat, especially at breakfast time. Grandmother would make pancakes for breakfast. She made them about two inches in diameter and I ate six. I was bragging to my mother about how many pancakes I could eat. She made me one the size of the skillet. That stopped my bragging.

As I have indicated before, we lived on the Pickerel Farm on Oil Spring Run Road. Quite often, a man and woman drove by the farm in their buggy, going to town to visit his parents and to buy groceries. My mother told me they were Harold and Daisy Smith. They lived up on Lemon Hill. One morning, the telephone rang. Mother went to the telephone, covered the mouthpieces, and listened in to the conversation. Harold had called his parents to announce that they now had a baby girl, named Hope, born April the 6th, 1922. Mother hung up the receiver and turned around to tell me this. Twenty years later, I married Hope.

On a beautiful sunny day in March 1924, Grandparents Humphrey came up the creek to the Pickerel House. We all climbed in their wagon and drove up Oil Spring Road, up the Jadwin Hill (long ago abandoned) and crossed the Martin Farm and onto the east side of the Harris/David Frash Farm, now DaySpring Farm. The reason for the trip was to inspect the farm with the view to purchase. My first reaction to the farm and especially to the house and gardens was "Why?" The garden fence falling down; loose tin on the summer kitchen roof; dead weeds and grasses all over. No one had lived in the house for several years.

My parents purchased the farm and after some house cleaning and big trash fires, we moved in. The next ten years were nothing but hard work for all of us. Fields and fence rows to clear. Plowing and planting. My parents were both hard workers. They knew how to delegate, also. There was always plenty for me to do.

Feed the dog (Tizz) and cat (Tabatha).[22] Cut weeds. Feed the pigs. Bring in the cows. Bring in

Figure 4. John with Tabatha the Cat

wood and kindling. We made it through the summer okay. In early August 1924, my mother filled out an order for two pairs of overalls and two denim shirts for school—first grade. The order went to Montgomery Ward. This ordering process continued for eight years as I went through the first eight grades of school[23] in the one room school at Triadelphia. We did school plays (such as The Drunkard) at Christmas time and the last day of school. Box socials were in, especially, if the lady schoolteacher happened to be pretty and single like Ruth Falconer, the sixth grade teacher. Ladies would bring a box of candy or cookies or pie or sandwiches. The box went to the highest bidder. The lady that brought the box and the bidder got to eat together under the watchful eye of everyone present.

June of 1926 was a month well remembered. Someone I did not know picked up Dad at the house. Two hours later, he came home driving a new 1926 Ford Touring car, four door. Total cost $418. What an exciting day.[24] The Fourth of July holiday[25] came and we all climbed in the Ford and drove to McConnelsville, out to

---

[22] "I have no recollection of where these names came from, perhaps the newspaper or radio." Tizz could be short for tizzy, as in "A state of nervous excitement or confusion."

[23] Among my papers are all of my "Teacher's Report to Parent" from the Morgan County Public Schools in Triadelphia, Deerfield Township for grades one through eight as well as my M&M High School Reports. In 1932, I placed 12th in the county on the eighth grade exam conducted by the State Department of Education (see certificate).

[24] It had three pedals: low, neutral, and high; reverse, and brake; see appendix 2 for more cars.

[25] The first fireworks I ever saw were on 4th of July 1929 on the Commons at McConnelsville.

Vignettes

Bloom Township, to visit Grandparents Richardson. What we had for dinner/lunch, I don't recall. When we were ready to leave, Anna Weaver Richardson had sugar cookies[26] for me, complete with tiny red ants.

I had trouble understanding Grandma and her German accent.[27] Grandfather was a gruff person. About 3PM, we started home. We hadn't gone far, until we were caught in a terrific rain and windstorm. Hail—trees down in front of us. A large tree had blown down in front of Uncle Vince's house.[28] Together, Dad and Vince cleared the tree, so we could go on home. When we got home, our house was intact, but one barn had exploded clear down to the foundation. The other barn was badly damaged. A lumber mill was brought in, timber cut and sawed, and the barn was rebuilt.

---

[26] See "Grandma Annie's Sugar Cookies," In Stacey L. Weaver, *Weaver Family Reunion: Treasured Family Recipes & Memories* (Portersville, OH: N.P., July 2006), p. 15.

[27] My father taught me, when I was ten, to recite the German alphabet.

[28] Uncle Vince (Vinson McKinley Richardson; Doc's brother) was killed by a "Large section of rock between post supports broke loose, crushing the miner, according to page 1 of the *Coshocton Tribune*, 23 December 1955, "Falling Rock Kills Worker at Mine [owned by Mr. Leavengood who had employed him for the past 14 years] in Linton Township" at 1:30PM on Thursday. Ironically, Vince usually worked as a night safety man, looking for fires, smelling gas, and listening for the roof working, which is a precursor to a cave-in, and looking for broken pipes. One of my earliest memories of Vince was his driving over to visit us and his bringing carbide to set off for fun.

John V. Richardson

Games We Played

We played several games during the fifteen-minute recess and lunch hour. Andy Over: We threw a rubber ball over the schoolhouse and the idea was for the opposing team to catch the ball. Softball: Our diamond was anything but level and the bases were a bare place in the grass. We had no idea how far apart the bases were supposed to be. I was the only student who had a bat, a ball, and a glove. The glove went to the catcher. Marbles: All the boys had marbles, but not many. I complained to my parents and Dad said "Make your own." I thought, "Sure!" He told me to go down the hill into the feed lot (down the valley toward Oil Spring Run). I would find a vein of white clay about six inches thick. He said, "Now, when you dig that clay out, make sure that you wash it so that you have only white clay." I took the clay, rolled it in my hands until it was nearly round, and then baked my marbles in the kitchen oven. They worked rather well as long as your opponent was not using "steelies." There were two or three of them remaining in the flat wall cupboard at DaySpring Farm in the late 1990s.

At home he must have played other games, including Old Maid, for after his death, we found a well-used pack of 31 cards from the Russell Manufacturing Company; and, we found five black dominos.

F.D.R. Closes the Bank

Dad told about how nice a man, Bob Miller, was to work for. My life interacted with Mr. Miller in a strange way when President Franklin D. Roosevelt closed all the banks for one day in the fall of 1932.[29] I had a savings account at the Citizens National Bank in McConnelsville. I had walked from M&M High School to the bank to withdraw some money so I could buy my lunch. The cashier at the window, told me, yes, I had money in my account, but I couldn't have it because the bank was closed. Looked open to me.

Figure 5. John in 1932

I told the cashier I needed lunch money—I was hungry. A well dressed man behind the cashier heard me talking, asked my name, and how much I needed. I told him a dollar would do. He handed me the dollar. I went home and told my parents this story. Dad said that was Bob Miller, President of the bank. I was impressed. The dollar was returned the next day. If I recall correctly, Dad and Mom seemed to have cash in the 1920s, but none in the 1930s.

---

[29] Actually, FDR declared the national bank holiday of 1933, closing the banks for a three-day cooling off period on Monday, 6 March 1933, shortly upon taking office after President Hoover; the Emergency Banking Act of 1933 passed Congress shortly thereafter. According to my Citizens Savings Bank Account Number 1586, I did not make any withdrawals between 22 July 1932 and 11 August 1933.

John V. Richardson

1929 through 1939 were Hard Years

The stock market crashed, the mines at New Lexington shut down, people were on the streets of Malta selling apples. I helped make hay for neighbors while I was in high school for twenty-five cents a day and lunch.

Dad could butcher. He would go to a neighbor's house with the butchering kettle, build a fire under it, scald and butcher hogs. In return, he got fresh meat. He did the same with beef. No money was exchanged. Labor and skill for meat. When we butchered, the neighbors came to help us. They, too, took home fresh meat in return. Eventually, Dad had shot so many cows and hogs that the .22 Savage rifle would no longer kill an animal. Pearl Weaver [Dad's grand-uncle, brother of Annie Weaver] sold or gave Dad their .22 caliber pistol, single shot Stevens with twelve inch barrel.[30] Meats were preserved by canning, salt curing, sugar curing, and smoking. Dad always waited until the weather was freezing. A quarter of beef was hung in the smokehouse (now, the Still Room at DaySpring Farm). For supper, Dad would take a sharp knife and cut a big slice (thin cut) and put it on a huge fork and hold it over the hot coals in the fireplace grate. It was delicious on homemade bread. In the fall, we made cider.[31]

---

[30] It is still in my possession, octagonal barrel, open sights, serial number 45958, Chicopee Falls, Mass, USA; no firing pin, missing the slide release as well as the extractor.

[31] Editor's note: After the death of my father, I discovered that they were raided during Prohibition; see "Twin City News Briefs," The Times Recorder (Wednesday, 21 May 1930), p. 10, col. 4. According to Morgan County Common Pleas Court Judge, Dan W. Favreau, if there is no entry in the Criminal Records (volume 3), then most likely the county's prosecuting attorney decided to enter nolle prosequi (i.e., "to be unwilling to pursue")--mostly likely due to lack of evidence (Favreau to Richardson, 29 December 2011).

Vignettes

Figure 6. Cider Press with 55-gallon barrels and sled

The Weavers (Dad's uncles) gave him a cider mill and press. He had a six horsepower Galloway gas engine [made in Waterloo, Iowa], which he belted to the grinder. Neighbors brought their apples for processing. He took cider in exchange. Then he took it to McConnelsville and Malta and sold it for ten cents a gallon. We grew sorghum for molasses and took it to a neighbor (e.g., Sparks or the Porters) for processing and he took some molasses for his work. I hated the taste of sorghum molasses and still do because it tastes green. Depending on the weather, February and March was maple syrup making time. Tap the trees with a brace and bit. Drive a spile in and hang a bucket on and hope for cold nights and warm days. The spile was made from a branch of a sumac tree. The pith could be pushed out forming a tube for the sap to flow from the tree to the bucket.

In September, we cut and shucked corn. My father loved corn mush. He would grate enough to make a pan of mush. After the corn got really dry, he would take the corn to the mill and have enough meal made to last through the winter. He also took wheat to the mill and traded it for flour. In early October, he would come home with a 100 pound sack of flour (four twenty-five pound sacks) plus 100 pounds of sugar. These were stored at the head of the stairs leading to the south bedroom at DaySpring Farm.

I walked to the one room school at Triadelphia for eight years then for three years of high school. The fourth year, we had a "new" gravel road past DaySpring and so the bus picked me up in front of the house. The spring of 1932, the new consolidated school building was started. I was the water boy at fifty cents a day for two weeks. After that I got one dollar a day. Big money. Well, bigger than ten cents a day for being janitor for the one room school. I cleaned the chalkboard, swept the floor, oiled the floors, fired the coal[32] stove, filled the water jug, and dusted the

22

erasers and desks. The money I saved, I purchased my first concertina for seven dollars and a half—no tax in those days. It was made in Italy with ten keys and two bass; I no longer have it; I wore it out.[33]

---

[32] I recall that in the 1920-30s, coal was dug from a seam on Willie Nixon's property, down on Island Run, just upstream before the creek crossing on T-1374, also called Frash Lane; later, the coal came from a Santoy coal mine.

[33] Elsewhere in this document as well as in an article entitled "Childhood Christmas Memory Brings to Mind a Concertina," (*Morgan County Herald*, 3 December 1997), I wrote about finding it in a Montgomery Ward catalog for $6.98. Sometime after 1939, I also purchased a golden pearl (standard or major) Parker Blue Diamond Vacumatic Fountain Pen [stamped 9]. See Glen Bowen, *Collectible Fountain Pens* (Gas City, IN: L-W Book Sales, 1982), p. 97-98 and Cliff and Judy Lawrence, *The New Official PFC Pen Guide* (Dunedin, FL: Pen Fancier's Club, 1989), p. 60 and George Fischler and Stuart Schneider, *Fountain Pens and Pencils* (West Chester, PA: Schiffer Publishing, 1990), p. 132.

Vignettes

Throw the Damn Bucket

The following narrative is a true story entitled "throw the damn bucket." It was mid-February and it had been raining hard. Dad met me after school at Triadelphia with our horses, Prince and Nance. The roads were muddy and walking as well as riding was difficult. I got on Prince and Dad on Nance. Prince was easier to ride, but more highly spirited. Under my arm was a lunch bucket with a glass jar and spoon. All went well until Prince caught his front foot in the mud and went down on his knees. It nearly threw me off, but I soon found myself riding a runaway horse. Every time Prince lunged, the jar and the spoon rattled and Prince gained more speed. Dad realized what was happening and yelled, "Throw the bucket...Throw the bucket...Throw the damn bucket!" I did, but I was in serious trouble. I had been guiding Prince with one hand and I pulled him into a ditch beside a woven wire fence. The two top strands of this fence were barbed wire. We came to a deep ditch at the end of a culvert, which crossed the road. Prince put out his front feet and stopped suddenly. I kept going, head first, face toward the fence. The wire shredded my overalls, but I didn't get a scratch. Incidentally, I crossed the ditch but Prince didn't. I was scared. I wanted to trade horses for the rest of the trip home. Dad wouldn't let me. I had to get back on Prince, but Dad had the bucket.

During the grade school years, several things happened that come to mind. As this text has been written, one thought triggers another memory. When I was seven or eight, one of our cows had a baby bull calf. She was way down in the woods. I found them and went back to tell Mom; Dad was gone. A rainstorm was coming up and we thought the spindly legged calf should be in the barn. We dragged the calf on a piece of canvas to the barn with the mother nervously following. Dad liked the look of the calf, all white and from good stock, so Dad kept him to breed our cows and others from our neighbors. The bull grew up and he weighed 1800 pounds before we had to sell him. The bull had been very gentle but we saw a gradual change until he was difficult to manage even with a ring in his nose. One day, Dad was trying to get him into the barn but without success. Suddenly the bull turned on Dad and chased him across the feed lot and got him down against the fence and was goring him. I was standing by the feed lot gate with a hickory stick in my hand. When I saw what the bull was doing to Dad, I ran to them; the bull was concentrating on goring Dad and he didn't see me coming. I smacked him on the rump and he turned to see what had hit him. That was when I hit him on the nose. He turned to finish Dad off but Dad was over the fence. The bull, head down and bellowing, then took after me, but I was bare footed and in overdrive. I crossed the feed lot, up the hill and over the fence. As I hit the ground on the far side, the bull hit the fence head on. I can still hear those oak boards crack. The impact stopped him. As I got up off the ground to run again, if I had to, I saw my Mother coming through the gate at the barn with the 12-gauge shotgun in her hands. She always loaded the gun and carried a spare in her hand. I could see the spare and knew there was a round in the chamber. Everyone and everything stood still for a few minutes. The bull got up and went into the barn very quietly. Dad had a broken rib, but that was all. A few days later the bull went to the stockyards. Years later, I discovered why the bull had turned cross. Neighbor boys teased him while he was out of sight from the barn (he was in a field beyond the barn. He liked to walk back forth along the fence, between our farm and the Clawsons).

One year, Dad purchased twenty-four fruit trees including apple, peach, plum, cherry and pear. The same year, we had one of the worst droughts on record; we lost many trees even if we did carry water from the creek. Sometimes the sun was difficult to see because of the dust storms, which started in Kansas. The next year (i.e., 1931 or 1932) was the year of the seventeen year locusts. Then, they took their toll. They stung the branches by piercing the underside of a tender branch to lay their eggs; these branches may then break off or become so stunted that they need to be broken off. However, several survived and we had fruit. Today (circa 1997-1999), there is one Kiefer pear and one Russet apple tree still surviving.

Vignettes

The Concertina

The childhood Christmas that stands out in my memory is that of 1931. Morgan County was already in the grip of the Great Depression. My family, living on the small farm just outside Triadelphia, never really observed Christmas. But families got together on holidays and that year my grandmother Harriett Hughes Humphrey gathered her children and grandchildren at her home north of Malta (overlooking the Muskingum River, at Tavener's Run).

My Aunt Stella Roberts (i.e., my mother's sister) and her family had come from Sandusky, Ohio. After Christmas dinner was over, they provided the musical entertainment. One of my cousins played a piano accordion. The instrument really caught my fancy; I had inherited my grandfather John Henry Humphrey's fiddle[34] and I was already taking violin lessons from Harry Whitaker. When I looked up the instrument in the Montgomery Ward catalog, I realized that I would never be the possessor of so grand a thing. Turning over a page, I found a concertina that was priced at $6.98. That, I might be able to afford![35]

---

[34] I remember John Humphrey playing fiddle songs by ear such as: "Fisher's Horn Pipe," "Devil's Dream" and "Soldier's Joy." Mr. Whitaker taught me the mnemonic "And-Eat-Breakfast-First" as well as "Farmer-Brown-Eats-Apple-Dumplings-Greedily" and to play "The Happy Dancers" as one of my first tunes. At Christmas 2007, I also remembered my father singing traditional ballads such as "My name is Charles Guiteau, My name I shall ne'er deny, For the murder of James A. Garfield [assassinated on 2 July 1881], I am condemned to die..." or "I leave my aged parents in sorrow for to die. But little did they think, while in my youthful bloom;" see http://www.fortunecity.com/tinpan/parton/2/guit1.html or Louise Pound, "Traditional Ballads in Nebraska," *The Journal of American Folklore* 26 (no. 102, October—December 1913), pp. 351-366 and "O dear mother, pin a rose on me, 'Cause there's two girls in the street you see....Chorus: Oh dear, oh dear, what ails me? Think what ails me;" see Jean O. Heck, "Folk Poetry and Folk Criticism, as Illustrated by Cincinnati Children in Their Singing Games and in Their Thoughts about These Games," *The Journal of American Folklore* 40 (no. 155, January—March 1927), pp. 1-77. On my concertina, I had the following play list: Mountain Wildflower, Skip to My Lou, Pennsylvania Polka, Red Wing, Red River Valley, Home Sweet Home, Oh My Darling Clementine, Onward Christian Soldiers, Goodnight Ladies, She'll Be Coming Around the Mountain, Carry Me Back to Old Virginny, Old Spinning Wheel, Rosewood Casket, Little Brown Jug, and Garden Gate; all of which I knew by heart.

[35] For more about this instrument, see James P. Leary, "The German Concertina in the Upper Midwest," in Philip Bohlman and Otto Holzapfel, eds., *Land Without Nightingales: Music in the Making of German-America* (Madison: University of Wisconsin Press, 2002), chapter 8.

John V. Richardson

I attended the one-room school at Triadelphia. That year, the teacher, Ernest Weaver, had hired me as janitor. For ten cents per day, I swept out and built the fire in the potbelly stove, which sat in the middle of the room. I saved the fifty cent piece Mr. Weaver paid me each Friday and by April, I was able to send a money order to pay for the concertina.

Soon, I had mastered the ten melody and two bass keys of the concertina. All that summer, Earl Scott who lived two miles over on the next ridge, would hear me playing and hike across to play along with his guitar. Sometimes, I would walk over to his house. Long before I had grown up, the concertina was worn out.[36]

During the time I was in grade school, I helped Dad in the field all I could. One day a week, usually on Friday, Dad sent me to the house to help Mom. "You might need to know how to cook," he would say. Mom baked pies, cake, bread, and churned butter for the weekend. She disapproved of working on Sunday except for final preparation of meals. Years after Hope and I were married, we think we figured out why Mom sometimes called me Joanne. When I helped her, I was Joanne, otherwise, John.

Money was always scarce, but game was always relatively plentiful. In the wintertime, we trapped rabbits, opossum, raccoon, skunks, minks, whatever came along. If a skunk was in the trap, I went to the house and let Dad take the skunk out (Dad didn't want me going to school smelling like a skunk). One time, a mink got in the trap. Little did I know that a mink had musk and would really spray a person. Talk about being sick and smelly. The trap line was on the bench trail on the west side of the road. The only deer I ever saw as a child was a picture in a book--now in the late 1990s, they are a nuisance.

---

[36] This text appears verbatim in "Childhood Christmas Memory Brings to Mind a Concertina."

The Airship Shenandoah

One time I was coming in from tending the traps and I heard this roaring sound. I looked over my shoulder and here came a huge airship. I hit overdrive and ran to the house and alerted my parents. It turned out to be the airship Shenandoah.[37]

Figure 7. USS Airship Shenandoah (Courtesy of Wikipedia Commons)

---

[37] This event occurred prior to 3 September 1925, and is well-documented by Aaron J. Keirns' Ohio's Airship Disaster: The Story of the Crash of the USS Shenandoah (Howard, OH: Little River Publishing, 2000).

John V. Richardson

The Violin

When Grandfather John Henry Humphrey died and his estate was settled, my mother inherited his violin.[38] He could play "Devil's Dream," "Turkey in the Straw," "Fisher's Hornpipe," and others. My mother's dream was that I become a violinist in a big orchestra (or a good doctor). A neighbor by the name of Harry Whitaker was a violinist and a music teacher. He charged fifty cents per hour for teaching music. Where to get the money? Another neighbor was a bachelor; he paid mother fifty cents a week to do his laundry.

Figure 8. Hopf Violin, first half of 18th Century (front, side, and back)

---

[38] In 1928, the violin had been sitting in an upstairs dresser drawer of the vacant Humphrey house and a mouse had eaten through the right f-hole; Whitaker, who lived in Triadelphia, repaired it, the neck having come unglued, and replacing the fingerboard by cutting and planeing down the original one. The bow was missing and replaced at that time as well. The so-called Hopf model from "a wide spread violin making family with their own model, the so-called Hopf model. The most celebrated violin makers of this family are: Hopf, Caspar. Klingental 1650-1711 (fl.) and Hopf, David. Klingental 1762-1786 (fl.). They made mostly trade goods of good and also poor quality. The tone quality is often very good, particularly those of David Hopf"; for more information, see Fridolin Hamm's *German Violin Makers* (London: William Reeces, 1961). The Smithsonian Institution advises that "The Hopf name is stamped on a vast number of undistinguished violins, an inestimable quantity of which are unauthentic" http://www.si.edu/Encyclopedia_SI/nmah/hopf.htm (accessed 16 October 2007). According to David Schlub of the Loft Violin Shop in Columbus, the violin is from 1800 to 1850 (interview on 24 July 2007).

Vignettes

I rode Old Belle or walked to take the lessons. In high school, I tried out for the high school orchestra and made first violin, second row, second chair. One particular night, Mrs. Edwards, our music teacher, said: "This is it! We will play three numbers and if you all do well, you will stay in the positions you are now in." Well, there was a young lady, Freda Almendinger, who was first violin, first chair. I set out to unseat her. I was watching my bowing and counting the beat. I missed Mrs. Edwards' "stop playing" signal. All of a sudden, I was playing a solo. Max Morrow, my buddy, kicked me in the shins and I stopped playing. Mrs. Edwards was furious. She broke her baton over the music stand, flounced off to her briefcase, got another one, came back and said, "John Richardson, you move back three rows." This event was just the beginning of my downfall as a musician. By the fourth year, I was playing obbligato. In this position, there isn't much to do, read ahead a little, if there is a water fountain nearby, go for a drink, come back and pick it up. I did get a letter in music[39] as well as glee club, though.

---

[39] Receiving a red capital M in 1936, my senior year.

John V. Richardson

Willie Nixon, the Bachelor

The bachelor mentioned earlier, Willie Nixon was getting older and decided that he needed some live-in help. He arranged for a local woman to live-in doing the usual household duties. All the neighbors thought that Willie was rich and it was common knowledge that he did not trust banks and probably had his money buried in the yard or hidden in his mattress. At any rate, he was found hanging from the rafters of the barn the next morning.[40] The sheriff and coroner pronounced it suicide, but the neighbors had other theories. (Grist for "Murder, She Wrote.")

---

[40] William F. Nixon (Oct 1870-2 September 1932), aged 61.

Morgan's Raid

In high school, I found myself studying ancient history. I complained to my parents and Dad said, "I will tell you some history that happened in 1863." Well, I considered 1863 as ancient, too. We stood on the front porch of DaySpring and Dad pointed across the road and into the distance.

Figure 9. Weaver Family House, Morgan County, Ohio

He said, "See that house? That is the Weaver house. Now, here's the history. July 23rd, 1863, General Morgan came through with four hundred cavalrymen. They were tired, hungry, and bone weary.[41] Morgan went into the log house and slept on the floor, protected by the big logs. Grandma cooked and baked all night, the troopers burned the rail fence to cook their meals and fed the newly harvested wheat to the horses. On leaving the next morning, General Morgan told Mr. John Weaver [being my great, great maternal grandfather] to saddle his horse and lead them to the Muskingum River and at gunpoint he did so. There are two stories about his escape and return home. Can you imagine the terror of seeing your husband and/or father leaving you at the farm at gunpoint?

---

[41] See "Morgan Raid File," now in the possession of the Morgan County Historical Society. See also, Lester V. Horwitz, The Longest Raid of the Civil War (Cincinnati: Farmcourt Publishing, 2001).

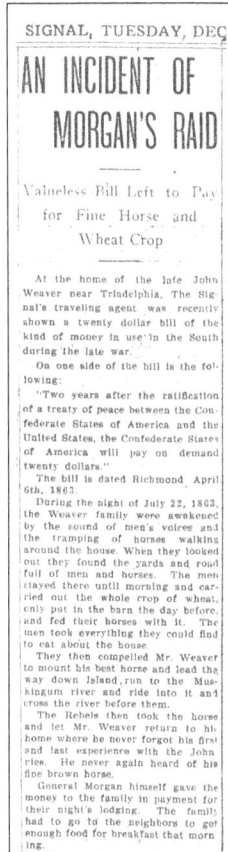

Figure 10. Morgan's Raid, 1863
Zanesville Signal (4 December 1906, p. 2, col. 4)

Can you imagine Mr. Weaver running back home to see how his family was?" My Grandmother, Annie Weaver Richardson, was eight years old when this happened. My father told me this story and anyone else that would listen. The Weaver log cabin is now at Dublin, Ohio (northwest of Columbus) and known as the Morgan House[42]--a great restaurant and boutique.

---

[42] Estimated in 1985 and located at 5300 Glick Road, Dublin, Ohio 43017; see http://www.morganhse.com/ (accessed 13 April 2009) which gives the misleading impression that the house somehow belonged to John Hunt Morgan.

Vignettes

Aspirations

I pursued the agriculture course in high school because if you were a farm boy, you were destined to become a farmer. I dreamed of going to college and becoming a Smith-Hughes agriculture teacher. But no one told me about scholarships. We had no money for college in 1936, my graduation year.[43][44]

Figure 11. High School Graduation, 1936

Despite my miserable failures in music, I graduated with honors. After graduation, I worked for the county on road maintenance, then a local feed store,[45] and learned to grade eggs at another store[46] that purchased eggs and cream from local farmers.

---

[43] Ernest G. Weaver, his elementary school teacher, wrote him on 15 December 1936 from Saltillo, Ohio: "I knew you would make good, and I know you would make good in college. I should like to see you go, for you are the type of boy who should have a college training; you would put your education to a good use."

[44] On Friday evening, 22 May 1936, I graduated with fourth highest honors among my other fifty-four member class, which consisted of twenty-four girls and thirty boys. At the FFA-FHA Banquet, I gave the Address of Welcome. On the 26th of May 1936, I was issued a "Certificate of Graduation" signed by James M. Turner, Superintendent, and Evelyn True Button, Principal.

[45] At the Quality Feedstore in McConnelsville as a salesman and truck driver from September 1938 to May 1940.

John V. Richardson

Visiting my Mother's nephews, Tom and Charles Maris, who lived in Zanesville, Ohio, was an education in itself. Of course, they had electricity; we did not. I was intrigued. In those days, the duplex receptacle was not on the market. Wall receptacles were just like the present day lamp base. For some unknown reason, I stuck my finger in one of those wall sockets. Boy, did I get it! This makes a good story: from this shock, I wanted to know about electricity!

Figure 12. Sightseeing abroad a Boeing 707 in Chicago during 1937

Coyne American Institute's Electrical School in Chicago had a big ad in a magazine. For $425, you could take their course and in three months get your electrician's license. I borrowed the tuition money from Coyne. Dad co-signed the note. To pay room and board, I went to the railroad yards of a morning at 5:00 AM. I was paid fifty cents an hour to unload freight cars. It was nice when I was assigned to a car loaded with fruit, especially California grapes. Somehow a hamper was dropped and before the cooper could get there to repair it, some of us had fruit cocktail for breakfast. I graduated with a point score of 92.5 out of 100 points.[47] I didn't take the examination for [the city of] Chicago because I didn't want to work there.

---

[46] On 22 April 1940, James Harris of M&M Produce Company wrote: "I have had John Richardson working for me off and on since 1936. He is conscientious and dependable man and he is a sticker on any work I have ever known of him doing. I would like to see him get in where there was a chance for advancement."

[47] I enrolled (Number 37FE1542) on 18 October 1937 and graduated on 21 January 1938 with a 90.2

Vignettes

Ohio Power, Philo[48]

I still couldn't find a job any place, so it was back to the feed mill. I put in an application everyplace that I could think of, but it was always the same answer—"Not hiring." Finally, Ohio Power, Philo Plant, called me. "Would I take a job in the janitor gang?" I jumped at the chance. Thirty-five cents an hour was big money. One of my first jobs at the plant was to get in a boat on the Muskingum River and clean the inlet where the water went into the plant. There was all kind of debris on the screens. If some of the debris got into the boilers, it could cause plenty of damage.

Figure 13. Columbus in 1940, AIU Tower

Local men were not happy with the Power Company because these men thought they should have been hired instead of that kid. They thought they should have been hired because they had families. My Coyne education had set me up for a job outside the plant. Coal to fire the boilers was purchased from the George M. Jones Coal Company about eight miles from the power plant. The coal was

according to my Coyne Electrical School Record, although my Diploma is signed by President Harold C. Lewis which says 7 January. While in Chicago, I lived at 1439 West Van Buren Street.

[48] "First re-heat generating plant, 1924 and first triple-compound generating unit, 1929" according to AEP at http://www.aep.com/about/history/firsts.asp (accessed 30 October 2007).

purchased on a BTU basis. In order to establish the BTU content, the coal was sampled every two minutes. Four electric motors and appropriate control equipment drove the sampling equipment. I ran and maintained this equipment. This job in the Chemistry Laboratory at Ohio Power lasted until March 13th, 1941 when I enlisted at the Columbus Barracks (aka Fort Hayes) in Columbus, Ohio.

The Draft[49]

My draft number had come up. One of the first to be called from Morgan County, I was sent to Ft. Riley, Kansas and started thirteen weeks of basic training in the horse cavalry. Weeks later, I was transferred to the mechanized cavalry because the Army realized that horses were outmoded. These were the days before Pearl Harbor and our active entry into World War II. The draft was for one year. The power company policy was—I would go and do my year—and they would have a job waiting for me. Five years later, I walked into the boss's office. He looked at me and said, "John that was one hell of a long year." I admitted it was.

Figure 14. Pencil Portrait by James Caldwell of Kansas City, 1943

---

[49] See 11 x 15 inch brown and gold heraldic crested album of military photographs entitled "John V. Richardson, 1940-1944."

John V. Richardson

Engaged to be Married

During the time I was working at Ohio Power, prior to going into the military, I had been dating Hope Smith. In fact, we were engaged to be married and decided to wait until after that year was up. Pearl Harbor in December and the country's entrance into World War II changed our perspective. We were married April 2, 1942 at the Smith family home.[50] I was home on a three-day pass and a one day absent without leave. I got by with it.

Figure 15. Wedding Photograph, 1942

---

[50] Our marriage was performed at the bride's home by Ted H. Waller and witnessed by Harold C. Smith and Herman Richardson. For my birthday in July or as a Christmas gift, Hope either gave me a Movado "gent's" wristwatch (Movement/Caliber #150MN, Case 18528411730); it is inscribed "HIS to JVR | 1942" or my 14-carat gold ring with a ruby-colored stone; both came from Argo & Lehne Jewelers in downtown Columbus.

Vignettes

A.P. Hill, Virginia

I was stationed at A. P. [Ambrose Powell] Hill in Virginia. I was post electrician for the reservation and this place was where I first met [Major] General George [Smith] Patton Jr. His artillery fire set the big pine trees on fire and all of the post personnel had to turn out to try to control the fire. He also had to have electricity installed in the camp site so he could show movies to the troops. Guess whose job it was to install poles, lines, set transformers, and take the power from the pole to the projector? By this time, I had gone from private to private first class to technician fourth grade. Shortly after this, one Major Kyle, post intelligence officer called me into his office and appointed me as an operator in military intelligence. Going to a movie in Fredericksburg, Virginia brought about the one and only result of this appointment. Dean [G.] Sandison and I had just come out of the movie when a big car with a Virginia license plate cruised by. It was loaded with more high tech radio receivers and transmitters than I had ever seen in one place. The license number was memorized and reported to Major Kyle upon returning to camp. Two days later, it was reported that a German U-boat had been sighted off the coast of Virginia. It finally came back that the automobile with the radio equipment had been communicating with the U-boat. What happened to the driver of the car and the U-boat, I have no idea.

John V. Richardson

Officer Candidate School

About the middle of April 1942, this same Major Kyle started a campaign to get me to volunteer to go to Officer Candidate School (OCS) for thirteen weeks at Fort Lee, Virginia. I was naïve enough to think I would get out of the Army soon because my year would be up. Finally, I gave in and went before the review board. Two majors, one lieutenant colonel, and one full colonel made up the board. They asked me only two questions: "if you were firing 75 mm artillery at that barn across field, what kind of math would you use?" I answered, "Trig." The next question was: "Which school you want to go to?" I wanted signal corps but got quartermaster.

Quartermaster was, at that time, responsible for supply and construction. My education and experience probably fit the Quartermaster better. They were

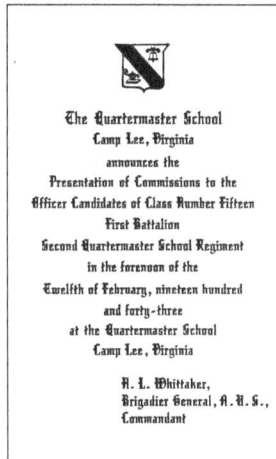

The Quartermaster School
Camp Lee, Virginia
announces the
Presentation of Commissions to the
Officer Candidates of Class Number Fifteen
First Battalion
Second Quartermaster School Regiment
in the forenoon of the
Twelfth of February, nineteen hundred
and forty-three
at the Quartermaster School
Camp Lee, Virginia

R. L. Whittaker,
Brigadier General, A.U.S.,
Commandant

Figure 16. Commission from the
Quartermaster School, 1943

responsible for the construction of posts, camps, stations, airfields, and roads. The construction was later transferred to the Corps of Engineers. OCS was pure hell from one twenty-four hour period to the next. The only "high" was when I looked across the breakfast table and I saw Dave Lowe, the president of the draft board when I was inducted. Well, yes, there was another point, a twenty-four hour P. K. doing pots and pans on Thanksgiving. Grades were given as either S for Satisfactory or U, Unsatisfactory. I made all S's and graduated with the class[51] (I don't know where in the class) but it must have been good. I was assigned as transportation and utilities officer to the 182nd General Hospital. This appointment was a 1,000-bed hospital. No one, and I mean no one, had ever heard of a Quartermaster, Second Lieutenant being assigned to a hospital. I was the envy of 380 new Second Lieutenants.

---

[51] Part of Class Number 15, First Battalion, Second Quartermaster School Regiment at Camp Lee, Virginia on 12 February 1943; see Announcement.

New Orleans

Two weeks leave, then to the 182nd Hospital at New Orleans, Camp Harahan and a Huey P. Long bridge. I had never seen such a beautiful bridge. The camp, enough said. I reported for duty and promptly found myself in the post hospital with scarlet

Figure 17. LaGarde Hospital, New Orleans

fever. What to do? The new Mrs. Richardson was coming down and no place to stay. You make friends quickly.

One Lieutenant Johnson knew of an apartment for rent. He rented the apartment and met Hope at the train. I told Johnson that he would recognize her by a big hat. She loved big hats. Consider the thoughts that Hope must have had when met by a total stranger and escorted to an apartment she had never seen. FAITH. The apartment was number nine, Fountainbeau Drive, New Orleans.[52] The 182nd trained for almost a year before we were shipped to England. That was a honeymoon year for the two of us; we enjoyed New Orleans: the Blue Room, Roosevelt Hotel, Arnaud's, and the Court of Two Sisters. We didn't have much money on a Second Lieutenant's salary, but it was adventure.

During this training period, I was called on to perform a special function. By this time, I had been transferred to the Corps of Engineers since utilities and

---

[52] This street is in the Seventh Ward — a sub district of the Mid-City District Area.

construction was now an Engineer function. Higgins Landing Barge Company was building landing barges twenty fours per day.[53]

Figure 18. On Lake Ponchetrain, New Orleans

The military brass wanted to produce a movie showing their use going onto a beachhead. I set up explosives and smoke bombs to simulate an invasion across a beach. I made a switchboard with three levels so that firing could be timed. The infantry stormed ashore and I fired explosives ahead of them and smoke behind them to camouflage their move. I never saw the movie.[54]

---

[53] See the New Orleans Public Library NUTRIAS collection re Higgins Industries Inc. and LCVPs at http://nutrias.org/monthly/june2000/june0018.htm ('On the Lake').

[54] In early 2007, I recalled more after seeing this picture: "I had gone all around the lake to set up an assault beach, making it as realistic as possible, using smoke bombs and M80s to simulate an attack landing. The 182nd men (and some nurses) went into bivouac for three days; the colonel declared the training successful and we all started back to the hospital. Crossing Lake Ponchetrain on the return trip, a storm came up, the lake became exceedingly rough, sinking a couple of the Higgins landing barges and drowning several men, none of them from our unit."

John V. Richardson

Duty Called the Unit to England

The 182nd General Hospital loaded on the Union-Castle Line's HMS "Athlone Castle,"[55] a British mail/passenger ship, converted for troop duty, in February 1944. Total troop capacity, 21,000. Nine lieutenants were quartered in a stateroom of about ten by ten feet, triple decked for sleeping. We stayed out of the room as much as possible. Being officers, we had better quarters and food than the enlisted men. Our dining room was

Figure 19. Union Castle Line's Athlone Castle

large. White tablecloths and silver to the right and silver to the left. Two meals a day.[56]

The staple was Brussels sprouts and fish swimming in sauce. I don't eat fish in sauce of any kind to this day. I didn't eat much on the trip either. As soon as we were out of the harbor in New York, we hit a storm.

---

[55] See the five inch silver spoon, hallmarked, from this ship, in my possession.

[56] See Union-Castle Line Menu: Breakfast and Supper for 29 March 1944 in my possession.

Vignettes

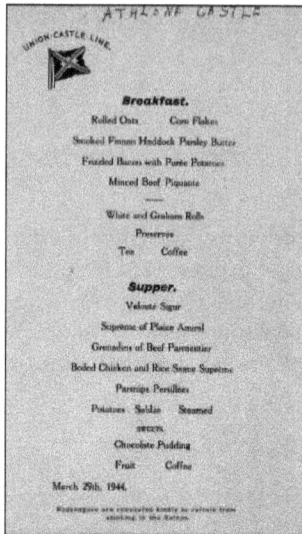

Figure 20. Ship's Menu, 24 March 1944

A storm on the North Atlantic in February[57] is a force to be reckoned with. I was seasick until we reached Liverpool fourteen days later. In fact, I was so weak that Lieutenant Gulley carried my duffel bag down the gangplank. The early part of the crossing was in the storm and visibility was zero. As the storm cleared, it became obvious that we were not out there alone. In fact, there were fifty-four ships in the convoy. One morning after the sea had settled down, we could see the escort ships change places. Then, all of a sudden, there were several large explosions. We could see sailors, rolling fifty-five gallon drums off the fantail. The drums contained high explosives. We were told that German submarines were following us. When we were about two days out of Liverpool, the anti-aircraft guns on the escort ships opened fire. We were told enemy aircraft had sighted us.

---

[57] The New York departure was 10 February and Liverpool arrival was on 24 February.

John V. Richardson

Communion Wine

The 182nd General Hospital had a total of 746 personnel. Among the personnel were three chaplains: Catholic, Protestant and Jewish. The Catholic chaplain was issued communion wine before boarding ship. One morning, he reported to the Colonel that someone had stolen a gallon of his communion wine. I didn't get any of the wine, but at this writing (24th January 1996) there are only three of us remaining who know who drank it.[58]

---

[58] Editor's Note: In September 2013, I found Chris Hass Clippinger and she heard the same story from her father.

Vignettes

Llandudno, Wales

Before I left the ship, I was handed orders appointing me convoy commander to lead the unit to Llandudno, Wales. Where is Llandudno?[59] "You will have an escort out of Liverpool and will be put on the correct road." When I stepped off the gangplank, my motor sergeant, [Winston] Graven, met me. He had been sent on the advance party to help make arrangements for vehicles, fuel, quarters, etc. for the main body. Talk about being glad to see a person you knew. The good sergeant had the convoy arranged in two serials (i.e., columns) with a sergeant in charge of each serial. We took off in the middle of the night, under blackout conditions, led out of town and headed in the proper direction (maybe). The last bobby we saw was at a roundabout; he said "go straight ahead to the next roundabout and deny yourself a left turn." Sergeant Graven said, "But, that's not the way I was instructed to go. And it's not the way I came in." All road signs and street signs had been taken down for fear of invasion.

Apparently there were supposed to be Bobbies at each major intersection and it would have worked if the last one we had talked to had given us "Go straight ahead." When we finally got to Llandudno, the rest of the advance party was in a state of panic. There is no way to describe how those of us in the convoy felt, especially the convoy commander. It's a wonder I ever made Captain.

We were quartered in private homes in Llandudno[60] until the middle of April [actually 9 May 1944][61] when we again went by convoy to a hospital[62] post at Sudbury, Derbyshire.

---

[59] A seaside resort and town in north Wales, Conwy County.

[60] The hotel, called the Summit Complex, had been taken over by the RAF in 1941 for a radar station.

[61] According to the National Archives document, Unit History, p. 13.

[62] See "United States Air Force General Hospital, Sudbury Record Plan (scale 1 inch equals 100 feet)" by Major A.M. Robinson, RE (11 October 1944), donated to the Derbyshire Record Office, England as D7082/1.

John V. Richardson

Figure 21. Sudbury Hall, Derbyshire

The hospital itself was a brick construction with a capacity of 750 beds. We immediately set up ward tents to raise capacity to 1000 beds, which was the 182nd General Hospital's stated workload. The hospital had general surgeons, orthopedic surgeons, medical doctors, a psychologist, a psychiatrist, dentists, sixty-seven nurses, two Red Cross ladies, and general medical administrative officers. Paul Hass was the Quartermaster Supply Officer; I reported to the Company Commander, Colonel Charles L. Kirkpatrick, Medical Corps.[63] At Sudbury Hall, I stood in for the Colonel many times at Sunday "tea,"—because it was a boring event.

By the time Operation Overlord (D-day) arrived (6 June 1944), we were fairly well settled in and I found myself with a multitude of jobs: post engineer, post fire marshal, post signal officer, post transportation officer, assistant quartermaster officer, and assistant medical supply officer.[64]

---

[63] On 25 June 1945, as a Captain, I received a commendation from Colonel Kirkpatrick for my superior work as Utilities Officer, especially for my "initiative, resourcefulness, and enthusiasm." More information about the unit can be found at http://www.med-dept.com/unit_histories/182_gen_hosp.php (accessed 11 September 2013).

[64] Still, I had enough days accumulated to take the train by myself to Scotland for three or four days of R&R and I had my photograph, taken at "Club Studios" in a kilt as a souvenir (see figure 21); while there, I learned to like bagpipes. From the lodge, a young woman in the ATS drove me in a lorry back to the station.

Vignettes

Figure 22. Dressed in the "Royal Stuart"
of his second-great grandfather

Under the Geneva Convention rules, medical personnel were not allowed to carry arms, but an engineer was required to carry weapons even if he was detailed to a hospital unit. Guess who rode shotgun for the monthly payroll with a .45 sidearm?

John V. Richardson

D-Day and then Battle of the Bulge

US Army Unit 182nd, General Hospital, located Sudbury, Derbyshire, 5 June 1944, 2350 hours. I had just returned from inspecting the guard and as I walked into the guard tent, the BBC was playing nice, light easy music. All of a sudden the music stopped. There was a pause and then the announcer on the radio said 'The Wine is Red' pause 'The Wine is Red' pause 'The Wine is Red' pause and the music started again. I thought this was strange, but the following morning I had a hint that it had some relation to the invasion because as I was going back to my office instead of the guard tent, I heard a heavy rumble, and turned around, and looked at the sky.

The morning of D-day[65] (6 June 1944), the sky was full of aircraft, small planes, large planes, fast planes, slow planes, and gliders being towed. Mid-morning, they started coming back--some of them on one engine, some on fire--some with holes in wings and fuselage and some went down near us.

Mid-morning, General Kirkpatrick called his staff together and announced "D-Day is here. Be prepared to take 400 casualties on short notice." While we were discussing this requirement, I called a sister hospital and got all the ambulances and trucks that they would lend me. When the call came, we had twenty ambulances and fifteen trucks. We had no idea of the ratio of litter to walking wounded patients. As the wounded were unloaded from the train, we sent the ambulances and trucks immediately to the hospital for processing. Four litter patients per ambulance and twenty walking wounded per truck.

It would be the world's biggest understatement if we thought we knew what to expect as the patients came off the train—hands, arms, feet, legs, eyes, face mangled or missing. With some, you could see the heart beat through layers of gauze. The smell of burned human flesh is a smell that is never forgotten. We learned eventually to identify the tankers, infantry, and engineers by the type of

---

[65] "On 10 May 1965, I was seated in a class at Fort Leavenworth, Kansas, attending Command General Staff College (see framed Diploma). Any Lieutenant Colonel who wanted to be promoted to full Colonel had to attend the school. We were in the last day of the school and we were required to critique several things that had happened in World War II; all of the sudden, the music on the public address system stopped; the announcer said 'The Wine is Red" — pause — 'The Wine is Red' — pause—'The Wine is Red'. I perked up because I had heard this before; curious about what it meant. The instructor took over the class and told us that this was a message sent to the French underground for them to destroy radio stations, bridges, railroad bridges, set up barriers, anything to help stop the Germans rushing to head off the invasion."

wound. Tankers were burned; infantry men shot through; and the engineers had feet and legs missing.

We continued receiving casualties until we reached capacity at 1,000. Then, came the Battle of the Bulge. The usual staff meeting, but I could tell the Colonel was more than a little tense. I knew why, when he said, "Be prepared to take 800 more on short notice." Somehow, it's like being there again.

I asked permission to use the Colonel's telephone, lifted the receiver, and Sally the English telephone operator answered (she worked for me), "Get me Captain [Blank] at depot G-18." "Yes sir, Captain Richardson." "We are to receive several more patients and we must expand the hospital by use of our hospital tents. I need the use of two D-8s and four dump trucks." His answer was, "Come and get them, John." My answer was, "We are on the way."

We surveyed, graded, erected tents, and installed lighting and double- decked beds. We finished the last tent as the trains arrived. This was an around the clock operation.[66]

---

[66] I was issued two certificates for captured enemy equipment on 16 November 1945: 1) Typewriter, German, Continental, Serial No. 692490-1 which Hope used to type the church bulletin for decades and 2) one pistol, caliber .37, Serial No. 175164 [possibly gray and Italian] which I sold to a colleague at Jeffrey Mining and Manufacturing.

John V. Richardson

The Sewer on the Medical Ward

Another "round the clock" was Christmas Eve 1945. The sewer on the medical ward side had stopped up and backed sewage into all the commodes and lavatories. We tried snakes, but that didn't work. We took the mobile fire pump and by-passed the sewage until we could dig a hole, twelve feet deep where we thought the blockage was. When we discovered the cause of the problem, we found a pair of nurse's panties.

The next morning I presented them to Major Larson, the chief nurse. She had been riding me to get the sewer fixed. I thought she deserved to see what caused so much trouble. When Colonel Kirkpatrick heard this, he called me in and said, "Now Rich, don't you do anything like that again." But I swear there was just a hint of a smile on his face.

More than once, I walked with the Colonel or Major Vaughn Herrin as they presented ribbons or medals. They presented and I carried the trays of medals.

During the war, I had the opportunity to be in London many times.[67] It seemed every time I was there, the Germans were there with their bombs. First it was the V-1 rocket and later the V-2 buzz bombs.[68] The V-1 sounded like a motorcycle. When it stopped running, you had better be under cover. The V-2 made no sound until it exploded. One thousand pounds of explosive makes a big bang.

When the war in Europe was over, we shipped the patients to the States and the 182nd General Hospital was deactivated. Some personnel were sent to the

---

[67] I purchased at least two souvenirs: A. F. Brown's "Westminster Abbey Snaps," which included twelve unnumbered scenes plus twelve numbered scenes from St. Paul's Cathedral.

[68] "Ironically, I was there for an unexploded bomb school as the officer from the 182nd General Hospital; I still have a souvenir piece of one bomb on which is inscribed: 'Marble Arch | March 18, 1945 | 0845.' On my way to the school, I heard the sirens and started running for shelter and a piece passed me and landed in a tree nearby." This Sunday morning attack killed three people; another eyewitness account by William Allan of Glasgow can be found in the 4 December 2008 issue of *The Daily Telegraph* entitled "Britain at War: V2 Rocket Explosion in Hyde Park." By the way, V stands for Vergeltungswaffe or retaliation weapon, consisting of a takeoff weight of more than twelve tons and forty-six feet in height; its impact speed may be nearly 3,000 MPH (see http://www.v2rocket.com/start/makeup/design.html, accessed 5 January 2009) and the last attack on London was 27 March 1945.

Vignettes

Continent to hospitals; others reassigned to the south Pacific for duty. Engineers being in charge of posts, camps, and stations, I found myself returning reverse lend lease property back to the British.

I came home on a small ship whose captain was General Wainwright's son. We left in January 1946 and arrived in New York in mid February.[69] It took us twenty-seven days to cross. We were driven off course due to a storm in the north Atlantic. We came past Bermuda; weather there was beautiful, sunny and warm. Most of us were on deck looking down at the bottom of the ocean, the water was so clear. Someone on shore was signaling in Morse code. We soon found out that they were saying, "Get farther out." We grounded and had to wait for the high tide to take us off the sand bar. When we passed the Statue of Liberty, I swore I would never leave the United States again, but I did in 1976.[70]

I was released from active duty, February 8th 1946 at Indian Town Gap, Pennsylvania. At the same time, I accepted a commission as Captain, Corps of Engineers, Reserve. At the time, I was absolutely sure that the next war would be with Russia in two or three years. I had no intention of going through OCS or of being drafted again.[71]

Thankfully, we never got in a shooting war with Russia. Being wrong in this case was good. The Korean War was a close call. In 1951, the Pentagon decided at the last minute that the 415th Engineer Brigade was too large a unit to be useful in Korea.[72] We all breathed a sigh of relief when we were told that. However, some officers were called to active duty individually due to special qualifications and needs. I had risen to the rank of Lieutenant Colonel by this time and was Chief of Operations.

---

[69] I believe that I returned on the SS Pomona Victory, a victory ship built in California; for more, see Leonard A. Sawyer and William H. Mitchell, *Victory Ships and Tankers: the History of the "Victory" Type Cargo Ships and of the Tankers built in the United States of America during World War II* (Cambridge, MD: Cornell Maritime Press, 1974).

[70] I revisited England, Scotland, and went to France via Dover and LeHavre, returning to the US on July 24th. My passport states that I am five feet, six inches tall. I also visited Mexico on an Elderhostel program.

[71] "War time commissions were temporary ones, so I would not have kept my rank and would have to go to Officers Candidate School again or risk being drafted again."

[72] "By this time, I was a Major in the 415th as bridge engineer." He stayed in because he thought we would be at war with Russia soon and ultimately that he might make Brigadier General (Hope Richardson to John Richardson Jr, September 2008).

John V. Richardson

The Jewel Box (England, 1946)

The jewel box was made by a German prisoner of war.[73]   I was stationed at Southampton, England. My engineer work group qualified me as Port Construction Engineer with the 14th Major Port US Army.[74] There was always plenty of repair work to be done on the deck.[75]

This work was done largely by German prisoners of war. They were all on their best behavior. They wanted to go back home as much as I did. By that time, I had been in England for nearly two years.

Back to the jewel box. One day, my master sergeant asked if I would like to have a jewel box. Of course, I would. All I had to do was supply hinges and a lock. I sent the sergeant off to shop in Bournemouth. The prisoner proceeded to make the box from scrap lumber. I believe it is mahogany.[76]

---

[73] Little has been written about this group; see, however, William L. Shea and Edwin Pelz, A "German Prisoner of War in the South: The Memoir of Edwin Pelz," *The Arkansas Historical Quarterly* 44 (No. 1, Spring 1985):42-55.

[74] See Bernard Knowles, *Southampton, the English Gateway* (London: Hutchinson, 1951) for some more detail about the port and its WWII history.

[75] The G-2 at the Port asked me to take a brown, legal envelope (a "hot message") to Paris since I was already going for a [seven-day leave with] four-[travel] day[s] R&R around Christmas time. I delivered it to an apartment in the Embassy area where I met a woman, Madame Zanzanaria (sic?), who spoke eleven languages; her 13-year old son could speak seven languages. I did not release it until she could call somebody who arrived wearing a French uniform. While there, I stayed at the Red Cross [i.e., the Hotel Wagram, 208 rue de Rivoli, room 607, stamped by the Military Intelligence Service], and went sightseeing at the Eiffel Tower; and, I bought a new Swiss gold plated (20 microns) bracelet push-in clasp, measuring 7-1/2" by 7/8", made in Geneve in a blue velveteen box and some French perfume, perhaps Chanel No. 5.

[76] See Jane A. Kimball, "Prisoner-of-War Art," In *Trench Art: An Illustrated History* (Davis, CA: Silverpenny Press, 2005). The author calls the box: "a lovely German prisoner-of-war piece."

Vignettes

Figure 23. Inscribed "England, 1946"

We had 150 prisoners.[77] They had their own command structure. I treated them the best I could as prisoners—food, shelter, blankets.

One thing I learned is that if they claimed to be carpenters, they really were. The man that made the jewel box must have been a cabinet maker. Note the dovetail corners on the box.

Language was somewhat of a barrier. One of our men spoke German; he was used as translator.

---

[77] Most probably, they came from France offloading at the Royal Pier in Southampton.

John V. Richardson

Return to Civilian Life

At the time of discharge, a sergeant made some comment about the G. I. Bill of Rights—house, education? I took advantage of the Bill of Rights.[78] Two years at Ohio State plus it got us into our first house at 984 Joos Avenue in 1956.

When I arrived from Indian Town Gap, there was great rejoicing. Reunited with Hope after twenty-two months, parents, neighbors, all rejoiced some with tears, times of high emotions. I went back to Ohio Power at Philo to see what they had to offer as a job. They offered: a) operations, b) lineman on a hot stick crew, or c) draftsman at Canton. Turned them all down. Considered the offer made by Hope's Aunt Blanche and Uncle Otie Schilling to manage their farm. Turned that down and entered Ohio State in April 1946.

---

[78] Technically, the Serviceman's Readjustment Act of 1944.

Vignettes

Ohio State was Difficult

Starting college at age twenty-eight and out of school for ten years except for military type of schools, learning to study day and night, was most difficult.[79] One professor teaching descriptive geometry [which allows the representation of three-dimensional objects in two dimensions] had taught the course so many years in the same classroom that he had pits worn into the blackboard where he drew the lines for each of the problems. He could not understand why we had so much trouble understanding. I flunked the course [in Autumn 1946], took it again under a young instructor, his first class. I passed the course this time [Spring 1947[80]] and have used the concepts many times since. Many of the instructors were five to ten years younger than I was.

The engineering curriculum required a course in speech. I did the course [Speech 401 in Spring 1946] with a minimum of effort. The end of the quarter arrived and the combined speech classes met in one of the auditoriums. The professors had selected the best students in their class to participate in competition. I wasn't selected and was glad of it. However, after each of the students had spoken, the judges needed a few minutes to determine who the best speaker was. The Master of Ceremonies looked around and said, "The student on the aisle, ten rows back, wearing a red sweater, please come to the stage." I had studied calculus [actually, either algebra or trigonometry] all through the presentations, preparing for the final the next period. The M. C. asked the student body to give me a topic to speak on: "Why We Should Not Fight Russia." I spoke for fifteen minutes; when I finished, you could have heard a pin drop. I walked down the steps from the stage and when I looked up, the whole student body was standing. When the winners were announced and the class dismissed, I passed Miss Breeze, my instructor, at the door. She said, "I didn't know you could do it." I didn't either. I got a B for the course, if I remember correctly [he did].

---

[79] I withdrew from the College of Engineering at Ohio State on 5 January 1948 at the start of the Winter Quarter "for failure to maintain the required cumulative point hr. ratio of 1.7".

[80] During the summer of 1947, I enrolled in Industrial Engineering 419 "Elementary Machine Work" and I turned a brass inkwell in the possession of my son, John Jr.

58

John V. Richardson

Four Roses

One time when we were talking, my father told Hope and me that he wanted his roses while he was alive, not after he was dead. This occasion occurred ten or fifteen years before his death. Christmas time rolled around and we were trying to think of something to give him that he would use. We decided on a fifth of Four Roses [a Kentucky straight Bourbon whiskey distilled in Lawrenceburg since 1888].

Figure 24. Four Roses

This gift was to become a family tradition. He would take one sip each day. When Christmas rolled around the next year, he had a few sips left. He liked a cold beer on a hot summer day, but one was enough. He knew the results of alcohol because his father was an alcoholic. He had to put the farm in grandmother's name, so they wouldn't lose it. Dad made homebrew once after Prohibition was lifted, but Mom didn't think much of the idea so he shifted to making root beer [requiring baker's yeast and sugar].

Vignettes

Jeffrey Mining and Manufacturing[81]

My wife, Hope, worked for Preston Cooke, a local realtor, and the G. I. Bill kept us going for two years.[82] It was time to start a family, buy furniture, and find a house. I interviewed at Battelle Memorial Institute[83] and was offered a job in fuels research, especially coal, at $250 a month. I turned it down because of my limited education; I could see no future for me. I thought I needed a doctorate.

Columbus and Southern Ohio Power offered $225 a month in commercial sales. Jeffrey Mining Machinery Company offered $225 a month in the engineering department as a draftsman. I took it. I knew I could do the job; the people were nice; and the company had a reputation for promoting for performance. I started March 1st 1948 and retired March 1st 1982 after thirty-four years.[84] Seventeen years were spent in engineering from draftsman to group leader to assistant to the chief engineer. Then I went on from engineering to marketing,[85] from field service manager[86] to factory service manager[87] and then to general service manager.[88]

---

[81] Apparently, Professor A. F. Puchstein, a specialist on electric motors at the Ohio State University, gave me a job lead; see employee number 7108. In my possession are two J-shaped copper items: numbers 382 and 462, issued by the Time Department. According to Hope Richardson in September 2007, up until this heart attack in 1973, he wanted to become a Vice President at Jeffrey, despite the fact that all of them were named Jeffrey. See "The Jeffrey Manufacturing Company: An Iconic Columbus Company" at http://www.jeffreyplace.com/aboutjeffreyplace/history.cfm (accessed 29 October 2007).

[82] I also worked for Hilltop Electrical Company from July 1946 to March 1948 (part time until 18 December 1947, then full-time). Around the same time, I started the application for a certificate of competency as an electrical contractor in Columbus, but did not file it.

[83] A private, not-for profit agency, devoted to science and technology, which opened in 1929 following the 1923 probated will of Gordon Battelle, who inherited his money from his father's steel industry.

[84] Bonuses ranged from $200 to $3000; one was spent on an Omega Ladymatic Caliber 660 (Case Number SS5303/08847, Movement Number 32364034) in a 14K gold filled case in 1968-1974 for my wife, Hope.

[85] I also found time to help organize the Boy Scout Troop 30 in the early 1960s; I recall one time at the Camp Lazarus winter camp when the eggs for French toast froze and I broke camp for warmth.

[86] "In recognition of your promotion to Field Service manager, your salary has been increased to

John V. Richardson

Figure 25. Heliminer (aka Coal Mole), 1969

On 23 March 1973, I found myself at the Charleston Memorial Hospital[89] with a heart attack. Spent three weeks there plus three months recovering at home.[90] Upon return to work, I was reassigned as training director as well as being in charge of parts books and maintenance manuals. Finally, I developed a training staff of three plus a secretary.

$1,050.00 per month," according to R. T. Hair of the Jeffrey Manufacturing Company, dated 29 July 1968; the public announcement appeared in the 1969 issue of Foundry, vol. 97, page 194.

[87] Circa 1969-1970, I prepared a nine-page report on the problems with Jeffrey's 120H Heliminer moving from prototype to production: bearings in the tram case, clutch parts, trim chains, and a clip or keeper (called a hair pin).

[88] Early in my career at Jeffrey, I invented a mustard paddle which could be used to spread the mustard by turning it upside down and removing it from the hole in the cap. I did not patent it, unfortunately.

[89] "CAMC Memorial Hospital is home to the nation's fourth largest cardiology program," according to their website at http://www.camc.org/CAMC/MemorialDivision/camc_memorial.htm (accessed 17 February 2009).

[90] In 2010, Hope S. Richardson wrote: "When he came home from WWII, he was smoking cigarettes...We were on our way to New Orleans on vacation when I discovered how many he was smoking: up to three packs a day. We were of course living on a budget but I told him then that if we could afford that expense then we could afford my getting my hair done every week...It was not something he wanted to do, of course, it is that smoking is so addictive. He did quit when Indian Springs elected him a deacon...He always claimed that the air conditioner "smoked" more than he did because he would put the cigarette down and it would continue to burn. But the summer his unit was in camp in Virginia, a helicopter was assigned to the unit. Dad had just alighted from a flight when a second officer climbed aboard; as they took off, the helicopter crashed, killing both men. Dad (understandably) started smoking again. After his heart attack, he was instructed to lose weight, exercise, and watch his diet. Also he was to stop smoking; he retorted that he already had stopped, "three weeks ago." And so he had! He never smoked again."

Vignettes

In 1974, Dresser Industries purchased Jeffrey. Business went downhill from then on because they could not sell equipment with the return-on-investment that Dresser required—33 %. The training department was closed and I was transferred to personnel. During the time in personnel, I held several jobs concurrently. I hired factory personnel; supervised worker's comp including managing the hospital; safety manager; safety shoes; food service; and security.

In winter 1981, we had spent a vacation in California, visiting John and Nancy, and when I walked into my office one of the nurses said, "John, have you heard the news?" And, I said: "What news?" "Management is offering a buyout." I went immediately to my boss's office and said, "Where do I sign?" It was a good move on my part because the retirement package was not bad; but some of my friends rejected the offer and two years later were fired without retirement benefits.

Concurrently with working at Jeffrey, I served in the Army Corps of Engineers Reserve. After thirty-seven years, I retired in 1978 with a reasonable monthly check and the rank of Colonel.

John V. Richardson

DaySpring Christmas Trees

Then, came the Christmas tree business in 1979.[91] The first batch came from John White at Six Mile Turn, over near New Lexington. They were regular twelve inches tall. I bought 100 of them; a mix of whatever he had to sell (what was left over) and I planted them up on "Long Point," along the fence line between Ormond Trash [Porter now, on the right side next to the road as you go back to Triadelphia] and us. They must be fifteen inches in diameter by now [early 2009]. I decided I would take the trees that did the best and replant. That turned out to be white pine. And, that's what I planted most of the time. I tried to buy those 1,000 at a time from the State of Ohio in Marietta; they have a big nursery down there. At one time, there were 7,000 trees in the ground—a couple of thousand of them are still in the Point Field (beyond the spring with the salt kettle).

Figure 26. At DaySpring Farm in the 1970s

You'd better start ordering in January; as soon as the ground is thawed, they will start digging trees and tell you to come and get them. I laid out the rows on ten foot centers, so a mower with a sickle bar would go between them. The final lot I got was a 100 from Penn State; an experimental fast growth, clean tree which didn't require much shearing. Rapid growth—I didn't see much rapid growth out of them.

---

[91] DaySpring (Choose-and-Cut Your Own) Christmas Tree Farm. I also wrote about this venture as *Uncle John's Christmas Story* (Columbus, OH: DaySpring Publications, 1994). Note that my "Journal" says on 30 March, I purchased 1,000 Scotch pine trees from Smith Evergreen Nursery in Magnolia, Ohio.

Vignettes

Figure 27. Shearing Christmas Trees at DaySpring

And you know the rest [i.e., last sales at DaySpring in 1997; closed DaySpring Farm by auction on 24 July 2004; we moved out of 614 East Schreyer Place in Fall 2006; moved into Wesley Glen Independent Living, 201 Virginia Gay, 5155 North High Street; then moved into their Assisted Living Plus in the summer of 2008, and finally the Health Center, room 219B].

John V. Richardson

Appendix 1. Obituary

John Vinson Richardson died at 2:30 p.m. Friday, March 13, 2009 after an eleven year battle with Parkinson's disease. The son of Sir Herman and Bessie Humphrey Richardson, he was born in Newark, Ohio on July 24, 1918. He is survived by his wife of sixty-six years, Hope S. Richardson; son, John Jr. and his wife, Nancy of Los Angeles; and special niece, Kim Yvonne Smith of McConnelsville, Ohio.

As an infant, John survived the great influenza epidemic of 1918. He grew up in Morgan County, Ohio, and graduated from Malta & McConnelsville High School, Class of 1936. He also graduated from Coyne Electrical School, Officer Candidate School, Command & General Staff College, and spent two years at The Ohio State University. He was in the first draft in Morgan County in 1941, pre-Pearl Harbor. As a full Colonel, he commanded the 364th Engineer Group at Fort Hayes, having served five years in active service and thirty-two years in the Army Reserve. He worked for thirty-four years as an engineer for the Jeffrey Mining Machinery Company. After retirement, he owned and operated DaySpring, a choose-and-cut Christmas tree plantation on the farm where he grew up.

John was a member of the Alum Creek Church, where he was an elder emeritus, following his service as elder for the Indian Springs Church of Christ for more than twenty years. Graveside service will be held at 10:30 a.m. Wednesday morning, March 18 at the Lemon Hill Cemetery, County Road #74, McConnelsville, Ohio. Adam Metz will officiate.

There will be a luncheon at the Smith Family Farm following the graveside service. In lieu of flowers, donations may be made to the Central Ohio Parkinson's Society, 1380 Dublin Rd., Columbus, Ohio 43215.

Published as:

"Richardson," Columbus Dispatch, 17 March 2009, p. B6.

"John V. Richardson," Zanesville Times-Recorder, 17 March 2009.

"John V. Richardson," Morgan County Herald, 18 March 2009, p. 2A.

Vignettes

Appendix 2. Cars, Cars…. And More Cars
By John V. Richardson Sr. and some John Jr. comments from 1963 onward

1926 Ford Model T Black Touring Car

Belonged to my father. He purchased it from the Ford Garage in McConnelsville; the salesman delivered it to the farm and Dad drove it (and him) back to town, then he was on his own (no driver's license was required then). I learned to drive by sitting on the seat in front of him; he worked the pedals and I did the steering and used the throttle. My legs were too short to reach the pedals.

One of our first excursions was to visit his parents in Bloom Township. There was a storm which left trees on the roadway; we had to remove them as we came to them. We arrived home to find that a tornado had come through, taking down one of our barns. The first long trip I remember, I came with Dad to the AIU building in Columbus, where he cashed an insurance policy to pay for the car: $416.

The car was black, a touring car with side curtains for inclement weather. It had balloon tires, 29x440. There were three pedals on the floor, one for the gears: low, neutral, and high; a second for reverse; and the third for brakes.

My first trip on my own was to town. I parked in front of a store which had a porch whose roof was supported by iron posts. I hit one and knocked it down. I went inside to tell the owner, who had seen me do it. The next time we were in town, Dad helped me fix it.

We only drove the car in summer. In the winter, it was up on blocks. One winter, I was working for Jim Harris, grading eggs, and I needed the car. To keep the radiator from freezing, I invented an overflow that captured the escaping antifreeze and recycled it.

John V. Richardson

1929 Chevrolet 2-Passenger Coupe

This was the first car I owned. I paid $50 for it from the Chevrolet Garage in McConnelsville after I came back from school in Chicago. It had a tan body with black fenders, a rumble seat and a spare tire mounted on the right front fender. It had a stick shift, 4-on-the-floor, foot-fed throttle, and a cut-out to by-pass the muffler. This gave it extra power and a great deal of noise. It repeatedly broke its rear axle. Although I became very good at changing axles, it was aggravating and so I traded it in.

My first date with Hope Smith, I drove the Chevy and took her to a movie. The next week, I bought a better car from Dimmy Walker, a mechanic.

1936 Ford V8 2-door Sedan

Black, 2-door, 3-speed on the floor plus reverse. I hadn't had it too long when the valve springs broke, hammering and smoking. Dimmy Walker replaced them; I do not remember what he charged. Once, I decided to clean the carbon out of the engine. I removed the nuts from the studs in order to lift the head, but the aluminum head had corroded so that it would not lift off; when I started the engine, it came right up. I drove this car to my job in the chemistry lab at Ohio Power in Philo. Fern Martin,[92] who lived in Triadelphia, said that she could set her clock when she saw me drive through.

I was home on leave soon after Hope and I had been married and I was taking her back to Columbus, where she worked at Curtis Wright. On Route 40 just west of Zanesville, we began having flat tires because of dry rot. New tires were not available during WWII. We had seven flat tires before we reached her rooming house just south of the university. I was able to repair the tires each time because there were inner tubes in each tire and I had a repair kit.

When I was overseas in England, Hope wrote to ask if she could transfer title to the car to my Dad, whose truck had finally worn out.

1940 Ford 4-Door Sedan

I returned from England in 1946 and entered Ohio State University. We lived on Patterson Avenue and were able to do without a car; at any rate, they were not available. When we moved to an apartment on Northwest Blvd., a car was necessary and I was able to find a used and well-worn one.

---

[92] Long time member of the Triadelphia United Methodist Church.

Vignettes

It was a black Ford 4-Door. Hope would often pick up Dede Laurrell, wife of Bob (who served in the 182nd General Hospital) and one evening when she did so, Dede's foot went through the floorboard. Dede (who had no car at all) said, "Just don't come for me again until you have a 'new' car!" Hope had taken driving lessons from a professional teacher and was driving by that time.

1949 Chevrolet StyleLine Deluxe 4-Door Sedan

At the intersection Cleveland Avenue and Joyce Avenue, semi didn't stop and rear ended the car, crushing the trunk lid. The insurance totaled the car and I bought it back from them for $50. Went to junk yard and asked for a lid and they told me what part of the yard to go to with my tools and he would price it for me. When I returned, another customer had my car jacked up and was removing the wheels.

1959 Rambler Cross Country Station Wagon

Forest green and tan in color. Purchased from Jack Brantner, my boss. Seats folded-down so you could camp in it. Seat belts installed because Grandfather Smith was towing a trailer to Florida and turned 180 degrees but survived the accident because they were wearing seat belts, according to the Highway Patrol. By the way, the drill bits untwisted, not being properly heat treated.

1957 Dodge (owned in June 1960)

68

John V. Richardson

White in color with bronze trim. Regularly parked in carport at 984 Joos Avenue. License plate: B884.

1963 Simca 5

White. Chrysler's import from France, designed as their cheap ($1495 retail) import killer. Bought it from Rex or Marietta Riggs. License plate: A364 (for Army 364th Brigade, for which he served as Commanding Officer). John Jr. got it for a combined Christmas and birthday present in 1969 and rear-ended a guy on North High Street, near Ohio State. It crushed in the left side headlight. On 28 July 2007, Melinda Miller told John Jr. that she remembered his teaching her to drive and hopping across the parking lot as she learned the clutch's friction point.

1964 Dodge 4-door (Pushmatic Transmission)

Vignettes

Aqua (blue/green). The first car John Jr. learned to drive in. Up in the new subdivision, he executed a three point turn in an unfinished intersection, but backed into the open sewer and cut the rear tire completely through to the rim. He changed the tire and went home. The Richardson's also towed the Nimrod with it to the Skyline Drive one summer.

1966 Dodge Coronet 500 4-Door Special Edition

First new car: a demo on sale at the end of the model year. Bronze color. John Jr. took the car to Carter Caves in Kentucky with friends (i.e., Mike Miller, Gary or John Kessler, and Jim Burnett) from church and they went to an outdoor movie theater and this guy leaving pulled into them as he backed up, scoring the right rear quarter panel. I got his name and address, but, of course, he didn't have insurance. And, then Mr. Ackerman, who lived in the neighborhood t-boned the car on Mother's side, which knocked it all out of alignment and it was totaled by the insurance company.

1970 Dodge Coronet 2-door 440

White. When you put your foot down, it took off; you'd better be hanging on (apparently, it could produce 420 horsepower). Didn't have power steering and it would wander off; wrong set of gearing in the steering column? Mom stuck scissors in the carburetor to get it to start—the automatic choke would stick. There was always some man around to help Mom out in a parking lot, but she would jump out and stick the scissors it and it would start right up. Gave it to Ron Cole, a member of the Church of Christ, who badly needed a car.

Ford LTD 4-door

Black. Based on a promotion, a raise in pay and got the use of a company car. Doc was living with us and he looked up and said, that happened to me once—somebody gave him a new suit of clothes and a new buggy. Jeffrey sold it to me for $150 when I retired in 1982.

Ford Station Wagon

150K trade in, from Ford Garage on West Broad Street.

70

John V. Richardson

1995 Toyota Corolla Four-door Sedan

Taupe color. The trunk had been damaged on the right side after being rear-ended on the way to church and it never quite closed properly. However, it has 108K miles on it.

Vignettes

Appendix 3. Prepared Horseradish Recipe

Figure 1. Horseradish growing at DaySpring in southeastern Ohio

Scientific name: <u>Armoracia</u> <u>rusticana</u> (related to mustard and cabbage; literally "strong root") and is a perennial in the southeastern Ohio countryside, the source of our horseradish. Other than the Bible (one of the five bitter herbs), the earliest mention in English comes from John Gerard's <u>Herball</u> (1597); in the mid-1850s, "German immigrants started horseradish farms in the Midwest."

1. Select smaller roots which are thought to be "sweet" while the main roots are stronger.
2. Clean the root (by scraping off the skin) and cut root into small pieces.
3. In a blender, grate, using a small amount of distilled vinegar (otherwise, the enzymes breakdown, becoming "unpleasantly bitter;" so, this step stabilizes the "heat").
4. Salt as desired.
5. If too hot, add a small piece of turnip, grated.
6. Pack into small jars and turn upside down to prevent darkening (that makes a good seal).

Notes: Prepare to cry! Use ventilation, perhaps a fan. My Uncle Ed Humphrey liked it on his ham; my son, John, and my daughter-in-law, Nancy, use horseradish on cured ham at Easter, which is also a common custom in Austria as well as Poland, Hungary and Slovenia, probably originating in southeastern Europe. By the way, it's also good in scrambled eggs.

SOURCES: Jan Lawver, "Horseradish," It's About Thyme 24 (no. 5, June/July 2006): 1 and 3 "Horseradish" at http://en.wikipedia.org/wiki/Horseradish (accessed 6 August 2007) and "Horseradish Information Council" at http://www.horseradish.org/homepage.html (accessed 6 August 2007); "John Gerard's Herball, 1597" at http://www.healthsystem.virginia.edu/internet/library/historical/rare_books/herbalism/gerard.cfm (accessed 7 August 2007).

Appendix 4. Pimento Cheese Spread

Ingredients:

1. One-half pound of extra sharp cheddar cheese.
2. One small jar of pimentos.
3. Three serving spoons, heaped, mayonnaise.

Steps:

1. Grate it into mixing bowl.
2. Open jar and add entire contents into bowl.
3. Add the mayonnaise.
4. Mix it thoroughly.
5. Store in refrigerator.
6. Remove in time to soften before using.

Created: 9 November 1999

John V. Richardson

Appendix 5. Prayers of Praise and Petition

In late December 2002, Hope S. Richardson published a small private edition of the following prayers of praise and petition. Since then, several people have expressed interest in having a copy, so these have been reprinted here.

1. Morning Worship Prayers

Lord God Almighty:

Look upon us. See the desire in so many hearts. We want to worship You and serve You.

We are thankful for Your love. You love us because You are a loving God, not because You find attractive qualities in us. Lord we confess that we are sinners. We pray for Your forgiveness. Give us the strength we need so that we do not continue in those sinful ways. Help us recognize and avoid sin before we commit it.

We thank You for Jesus, Your Son. Help us to know Him; help us to be more like Him in all our ways.

Thank You, Father, for all the blessings You have given to us. Thank You for blessing us with all that we need: food, clothing, shelter, our daily "bread." Most of all, we thank you for Jesus, Your Son and our Brother, who gave us salvation through His death on the Cross for us. Thank You for His resurrection from the dead, which assures us of our life eternal with You.

Here at Alum Creek this morning, we all pray for our members, especially for those serving on the Building Committee. We anxiously await the day when we can move into Your house. Help us as we strive to make this a reality.

And we pray for Your servant who will come to work with us here. We believe that You do guide us and will guide him as we decide to work together to further Your kingdom in this place.

We are blessed with Elders, Deacons, Teachers, and with Worship Directors who love You and are talented and willing workers. Continue this blessing for us.

Help us all to demonstrate Your love to each other and to this community, which You have appointed for us.

In the name of Jesus' Amen.

Vignettes

✝

Mighty God, Everlasting Father:

We come before You being thankful that we call You our Father... that we can put our problems before You and know that You hear our call... know that You answer our pleas... We can sing praises to Your name through Your Son Jesus Christ, the Son You gave up for us so that we have our sins forgiven. We need only ask. Father, we are thankful for Your love, for Your mercy, for Your grace.

Help us to understand that we must as a congregation form a firm relationship with You and with each other and with our community. Help us to show and to speak to others around us of Your love, Your Mercy, Your grace, Your wonderful gifts to each of us.

We ask for Your blessing on Bernice Strickland as she continues her recovery, on Norma Bowen, on Lynn Harris, on Gladys Damron, on Mildred Hayes, as they each continue their recovery. We pray a special comfort for Leo Parrish and his family in their recent loss of his mother.

We lift up to You our Deacons, our Elders, our Teachers, and Committee Members. Especially lead the members of the Building and of the Finance Committees as they inspire us to fulfill our intent for a facility to serve the Alum Creek community. We thank you for leading David and Susan Estes to join our efforts here. Bless our work as we all learn to labor together.

We thank You for Bill Renner who so competently and willingly explains to us Your message of love and forgiveness in this interim period.

God, through all of this, keep us aware that the new building we anticipate is not Your church - but it will house us who are Your church, who are becoming Your church at the Village of Alum Creek. And again we thank You for Your Love, Your Mercy, and Your Grace.

This prayer is brought to You through Jesus Christ, Your Son, and our Savior.

Amen.

✝

John V. Richardson

Adapted from the Prayer of St. Augustine

O Father:

We turn aside from a busy, noisy world, seeking rest for our spirits and light for our souls.

Father, we bring our work to be sanctified, our wounds to be healed, our spirits to be refreshed, our faith to be renewed. Draw us to You ... Bring harmony to us, and silence the discord in our lives.

We thank You for the leadership of our Elders, Deacons, and Minister, and each of our Teachers. Strengthen them as they instruct us all.

Father, Your greatness is beyond our highest praise. We thank You for Your Son, our brother, and for Your gift of life everlasting. We do remember Christ's suffering, His agony on the Cross ... And we rejoice and believe in His resurrection.

Father, You have sent us visions of the love that is in You, of the good that may be in us. We thank You, dear Lord.

In Jesus' name.

✟

Vignettes

A Paraphrase of Psalm 119

Let our cries come before You, O Lord;
    Give us understanding according to Your word.
Let our supplications come before You;
    Deliver us according to Your word.
Our lips pour forth praises,
    For You have taught us Your statutes.
    Our tongues sing of Your word,
For all Your commandments are right.
    Let Your hand be ready to help us,
    For we have chosen Your precepts.
We long for Your salvation, O Lord, and Your law is our delight,
    Let us live that we may praise You.
    And let Your ordinances help us.
We have gone astray like lost sheep. Seek Your servants,
    For we do not forget Your commands.

In the name of Your Son and our Savior we do beech You. Amen.

✠

John V. Richardson

Psalm 150*

Father in Heaven:

We do praise You. We have gathered here to praise You. We praise Your name in prayer, in song, in the reading of Your word, and in having it explained to us, yea, in our communion together.

We praise You for sending Christ Jesus to be our brother, to live among us, to suffer for us, to provide for us - if we but listen and obey - with a home with You. He taught us to endure and to hope.

We praise You, Lord, for all the blessings You bring to us: homes, families, food, all the "good" things of life. Yes, we praise You for the very air which we breathe.

We praise You for the leaders of our country as well as for our world leaders. May they each praise Your name.

We praise you for our Elders. We praise You for our Deacons and for all the leaders of our ministry system. We pray You will bless and guide each one of them.

Bless and guide each one of us as we preach the Gospel, Your Good News, to all nations. We praise you especially for Ed Kirkpatrick's missionary journey to Your people in India. We praise You for the small part You have allowed each of us to have in that work.

Thank You, Father, for blessing our sick. Keep us fast in the assurance that You are always with us, sick or well, poor or rich, faithful or not. We praise Your name.

We praise You, God.
We praise You, Lord.
We praise You, Father.

Through Jesus Christ. Amen.

*Hope S. Richardson used a slightly modified version of this pray on Sunday morning, 15 May 2011 at Alum Creek Church of Christ.

✝

Vignettes

New Elders

Our Heavenly Father,

Our Creator and our God:

To You we owe our very being. It is to You whom we pray.

Especially this morning we pray for our "new" Elders, for Weldon Abels and George Wooster. We pray for their leadership of us, that through them, we will better know what is Your will for our lives. May they initiate great works among us, to Your glory.

And now we pray, too, for ourselves, that we recognize what it is that we owe to these men. Help us to know them, each one of our Elders, each different in his gift, his strength, and his weakness. As men, they share with us in fears and frustrations, they feel joy and pain as each of us do, they are subject to sin and error just as we each are.

Help us to be sensitive to their needs as humans with us, but as our Elders, responsible for the safe delivery of our souls to face You and our Day of Judgment.

Help us to respect these men, Father. Help us to submit to them, not just when we agree with a decision as a proper one or one that appeals to us, but help us always to be submissive and supportive when they stand for You. Help us to show them our love, to talk with them, whether in support or in difference. Allow us to be diligent followers of their leadership for You. Cause us to be constant in our prayers for them.

As we are now.

Through Your Son,
Our brother,
Jesus Christ.

Amen.

✟

John V. Richardson

New Year

Righteous Father:

Great and marvelous are Your deeds,

Lord God, Almighty.

Just and true are Your ways,

King of the Ages.

Who will not fear You, O Lord,

And bring glory to Your name?

For You alone are holy.

All nations come and worship You,

For Your righteous acts have been revealed.

We know You kept Your promises to Israel. We know You will keep Your promises to us.

As we continue to try to preach repentance to all nations and peoples, we ask that You lead us. We are at a new beginning in the way that we mortals measure time as well as in our proposed new location. Lead us to concentrate on the important things: Love for You, our Sovereign God, love for each other, and love for those of the world.

Lead us to review our mission and to rededicate ourselves personally and collectively to faithfully fulfill that mission.

As we launch into the adventure of acquiring land and planning a building, give us great faith in the possibilities. Bless each one of us, and especially those who are our Elders and Deacons as they lead us forward.

God, we ask not because we are righteous but because of Your great mercy. Thank You for hearing our prayer...

✝

Vignettes

Thank You/We Remember

O Lord, let the words of my mouth and the meditation of my heart be acceptable in Thy sight, O, Lord, my Rock and my Redeemer.

Lord, we come together this morning as Your congregation.

We praise You ...
We bless You ...
We adore You ...
We glorify You ...

Thanks we give unto You.

We thank You for our food as we remember the hungry of the world. We thank You for health as we remember the sick:

Especially this morning, we remember our brother Chuck Dronsfield and pray that he will soon be able to be about, serving You as he is accustomed to do.

We lift up Rex Riggs to you. Rex has been ill for so long. Make his stay in the hospital comfortable. Give him Your healing.

Be with Norma Bowen and with Lucille Rucker ... and there must be others about whom I do not know. You know all things; heal us with Your own healing.

We thank you for freedom and remember the enslaved - our brothers in Poland and in other parts of the world. Give all peoples Your freedom, Lord.

We remember Jesus Christ and the freedom He brought to us. We remember His saying as recorded in John: "The fields are white for harvest." Prepare us to help with this harvest, for we are mindful of the sacrifice of Jesus. Let Your promise of eternal life prick us to remember that even our closest friends and neighbors have never accepted Him as their Savior. May this very congregation be "forced" into telling the Good News.

Father, we sin. We are keenly aware that we do sin. Forgive us. We pray You will avert us from evil, though it be the thing we have prayed for, and give us the good which from ignorance we do not ask.

God, bless us, Your children.

✞

John V. Richardson

A Paraphrase of Psalm 119

Let our cries come before You, O Lord;
      Give us understanding according to Your word.
Let our supplications come before You;
      Deliver us according to Your word.
Our lips pour forth praises,
      For You have taught us Your statutes.
      Our tongues sing of Your word,
For all Your commandments are right.
      Let Your hand be ready to help us,
      For we have chosen Your precepts.
We long for Your salvation, O Lord, and Your law is our delight.
      Let us live that we may praise You.
      And let Your ordinances help us.
We have gone astray like lost sheep. Seek Your servants,
      For we do not forget Your commands.

In the name of Your Son and our Savior we do beech You.

✝

Vignettes

Psalm 150

Father in Heaven:

We do praise You. We have gathered here to praise You. We praise Your name in prayer, in song, in the reading of Your word, and in having it explained to us, yea, in our communion together.

We praise You for sending Christ Jesus to be our brother, to live among is, to suffer for us, to provide for us - if we but listen and obey - with a home with You. He taught us to endure and to hope.

We praise You, Lord, for all the blessings You bring to us: homes, families, food, all the "good" things of life. Yes, we praise You for the very air which we breathe.

We praise You for the leaders of our country as well as for our world leaders. May they each praise Your name.

We praise you for our Elders. We praise You for our Deacons and for all he leaders of our ministry system. We pray You will bless and guide each one of them.

Bless and guide each one of us as we preach the Gospel, Your Good News, to all nations. We praise you especially for Ed Kirkpatrick's missionary journey to Your people in India. We praise You for the small part You have allowed each of us to have in that work.

Thank You, Father, for blessing our sick. Keep us fast in the assurance that You are always with us, sick or well, poor or rich, faithful or not. We praise Your name.

We praise You, God.
We praise You, Lord.
We praise You, Father.
Through Jesus Christ.

Amen.

✝

John V. Richardson

Prayer of Thanksgiving, Part I

Our Father which art in Heaven:

We come to Thee with our prayers of thanksgiving, for Thou art the source all that we have. We are thankful that we can call Thee "father," that Thou doest call us Thine children, even with our sins.

When Thou didst create the universe, Thee had a master plan for everything. It was and remains a plan for us to live by, guaranteed by Thy promise of everlasting life with Thee.

Thou sent Thy Son Jesus to us to teach us by his healings and teachings to love Thee and to love our neighbor. In so doing, we will preach Thy Gospel to nations. We thank Thee that we are entrusted with Thy saving message.

We thank Thee for those who have come before us, who taught us Thy ways. For our mothers and fathers, our grandmothers and grandfathers, for all generations unto this day. For our preachers and teachers, the elders who have guided us and taught us to love Thee and our neighbors, to follow Thy plan for our lives.

And now we pray: " May those who come behind us find us faithful. May fire of our devotion light their way. May the footprints that we leave lead them believe, and the lives we live inspire them to obey. May all who come behind find us faithful..."

Note: This prayer was part of a 3-part prayer, praising God for generations past, those who came before us. Another prayer thanked God for present generations and yet another was for our future teachers and leaders.

✝

Vignettes

Millennium Prayer for Morning Worship

We come to You with thanksgiving in our hearts for the abundance with which You have provided us. Forgive us for the times we take for granted all of our many blessings. You provide food, clothing, shelter, family, loving friends. But most of all, we thank You for Your Son, Jesus Christ. We thank You for leaving Your Spirit until Your work on earth is done. Help us to be more aware this great blessing.

We pray that we will proceed with Your work in the way that You would have us do it. Let us -and all mankind - learn to work together in peace and harmony. We thank You for the progress being made in our plans for a place of worship, and for the progress in our fund raising.

We thank You for our leaders here at Alum Creek, for our elders and deacons, for those who teach us and our children, for each committee member, for each small group leader. Guide us always in Your ways.

This morning, our hearts go out to those of our number who are hurting. Please bless those who are ill, who are shut in, who are lonesome, who are tired. Bring to each, Your perfect peace and a great strength of faith. Bless us each with physical well being. Heavenly Father, Creator of the Universe

Lord God, as man tells time, this is our new year, a new millennium. Thank You for our safe entry into this period. Guide us as we work our way down this new highway.

Thank You for the comfort of our knowledge that You do hear and answer .our prayers. Open our ears to hear Your answers.

✠

John V. Richardson

Morning Prayer, September 26, 1999:

To my family here at Alum Creek, I say, in the words of Paul, "Grace to you from God our Father and the Lord Jesus Christ."

Prayer

Father, we are called together this morning to worship You. Hear our prayer as we know You do.

You are the source of all goodness, of life, light, health, and knowledge. Thank You for all that You have given us so lavishly: food, shelter, life, love.

We thank You for those who have loved and cared for us... Fathers and mothers, sisters and brothers, husbands and wives, children and grandchildren, friends and neighbors. Your care for us is manifest through them.

This morning, we thank You for the progress that Lynn Harris has made since her successful surgery. Bless all our sick as You have blessed Lynn and her family.

Lord, we are continually amazed that You have allowed mankind to discover so many ways of prolonging our lives. It is miraculous. Not the miracle that Jesus performed while He walked on the earth, but a miracle of our day and age. All power is Yours!

Thank You, Father. You forgive us when we forget You. When we fall, You pick us up and mend us. just as a mother bird shelters her young with her wings, You shelter us with Your love and caring. You are ever present, in our darkest nights and in our brightest days. Help us to remember You, to ask for comfort in times of trouble, to give You praise in the times of blessing, when You rejoice with us.

Your Alum Creek family has been called to build a house of worship and service. We feel keenly our need for Your guidance as we proceed in this adventure. Help each of recognize our own talents and, yes, those of others, so that we can work together effectively.

This morning, we pray for a special blessing for our Elders. For Val Harris as he struggles to lead us even as he suffers family concerns. For Judge Conniff as he labors among us while embarking on a new course for his own life. So too do we pray for our Deacons, Teachers, and Special Ministries - for the Building Committee, the Finance Committee, the Preacher Search - for all our efforts to serve You.

You do bless us, and we thank You. Through Christ Jesus, Amen.

✟

Vignettes

Note: After four years of Sunday morning meetings at the Alum Creek Elementary School the congregation of Alum Creek Church celebrated their move into the new building at 6256 South Old State Road, Lewis Center, Ohio. This First Sunday celebration, which invited other congregations and donors to the Capital Campaign to join with us, was held on August 11, 2002.

Ecclesiastes, Chapter 3, verse 1
"There is a time for everything, and a season for every activity under heaven."

Our Lord, our Rock, our Redeemer - Most High:
We have come to this time and this place to praise You and give You thanks for specific blessings, for we know that all we are and have comes from You.

You have heard our prayers and blessed our vision for the four years that we planned to build this house. Today, we celebrate its fulfillment. It was by your Grace that we have accomplished this. Thank You, Lord; we praise You.

Lord God, You have blessed us from the beginning. You sent to us a young enthusiastic preacher and his helpmate. We have Elders and Deacons who give us spiritual leadership: They are following You. They look to You for direction. Thank You for these men. We thank you for Committee Chairs and Committee members, for their abilities and their sharing of time and talents. Our congregation has many gifted members; we praise You for bringing them here to Alum Creek.

We praise and thank You, God, for the confidence we have that You will be with us as we continue the journey we have begun here.

Only recently, Father God, we have witnessed Your love and healing power during days of illness and distress. We praise and thank You for Your loving care. We know You are always with us and we thank You, Lord.

We praise You most of all, God, for sending Your Son to provide us salvation through His sacrifice.

May Your Grace and Peace reign over Your people here at Alum Creek.

✝

John V. Richardson

Computer

Consider your computer.

Let us pick up the mouse and x out of the program we are currently working on. Clear the screen.

Clear our minds of all thoughts: ... about what's for dinner, how the roast is doing. ... who's winning the election. ... whether the stock market is failing. ... how many months the job will survive. ... the Christmas decorating and shopping still to be done. ... who is preaching this morning.

Now - Next move: look over to the left side of the screen and click on the icon that looks like a cross; beneath it, the name "Jesus."

This part of our worship is about remembering Jesus Christ. First, think about how and why Jesus was sent to the earth.

One evening last week, Hope was reading a bedtime story to me. She was downloading from Max Lucado's book, Cosmic Christmas.

Two ideas struck me before I logged off. God has given me two gifts. He gave me freedom of choice. Adam and Eve blew that. By making a wrong choice, they sinned in a big way. They chose to belong to Satan. To whom do I belong?

Then God gave me a second gift: Immanuel, Jesus. One who died for my sins.

We have made our choice and we belong to Jesus, our brother who died on the Cross. Just before He was crucified, He feasted with the Disciples, a celebration. And then He said, "This is the way I want you to remember Me." He took the bread, saying, "Take. Eat, this is my body." He also took the cup, and, giving thanks, said, "Drink ye all of it for this is My blood of the covenant, poured out for the forgiveness of sin."

God moved some of His people to record His instructions and they are handed down to us in the Scriptures. We follow His instruction today.

Bread:

Father, we break this bread in memory of Jesus and all the gifts You send to us. We thank you.

Wine:

We remember You and Your Son Jesus as we drink this cup in His memory.

✝

Vignettes

Renewal

Loving Father:

It is a blessing to speak to You in prayer. You are always there for us, whenever we approach You.

We praise You for Your forgiving nature, for You gifts of grace and peace.

We praise You for Your great plan of springtime renewal. We praise You for all Your creation. You are a great and awesome God.

Help us as we try to make Your word known in this community through our lives and our teachings here.

As always, there are many sick among us. We are weak and feeble and sinful. Send You messengers among us that we might be witnessed to and encouraged in all of Your ways. Be especially mindful of all who are named in our bulletin, and whatever our physical condition, keep us faithful to You, spiritually healthy.

Eternal Father, we praise You for blessing Alum Creek with so many committed and untiring Christians. Bless each elder - Randy Lucas, Val Harris, Judge Conniff - as they watch for our souls.

Be with each deacon and each teacher (especially David Estes), and with each committee member. May we ever work together in harmony.

Daily, we remember Your Son, our brother, Jesus Christ. We thank You for this incomparable gift. Your blessings upon us are eternal. Thank You.

✝

John V. Richardson

2. Communion Prayers

What if Jesus walked into this room this morning? Would we recognize him? I don't know.

Would we be like the two men on the road to Emmaus (Luke 24:13)? They walked along discussing the wonderful events of the last few days. Then Jesus came along ... they didn't recognize him.

Would He have to remind us of all that He has done for us? I don't know.

Let us remember His sacrifices and His gift to us as we break bread together. He did this with His disciplines; He does it with us today.

BREAD:

Living Lord: We thank you for Your Son, our Savior. We break this bread together in memory of Jesus. Bless this bread and bless us as we partake of it.

WINE:

Father, bless this fruit of the vine as we drink it in memory of Jesus, our Savior.

GIVING:

Thank You for blessing each of us so bountifully. You supply all of our needs. May we give back with the same love You have given us.

✠

Vignettes

"Christ Triumphant Over Sin & Death"

Thursday, Hope and I toured the "Art Alive" show now at the Art Museum. I was getting tired so I found myself a gallery with a nice upholstered bench and sat down. When I looked up, straight ahead of me was a very startling painting, life sized, of a pleasant looking man. He seemed to be loving and forgiving, a man you'd like to know.

I couldn't read the title from that distance, but I found clues: There were nail holes in His hands and feet, and a wound in His side. A piece of white cloth was falling away from his body, and angels were ministering to Him. His foot was firmly on a serpent pinned to a skull. There was a fire in the lower corner, but He held a staff with a pennant, pointing up.

The title was "Christ Triumphant Over Sin and Death."

Seeing this made my day. Because Christ Jesus has won victory over death for each of us.

Bread:

Father, bless us as we give You thanks for this bread as it represents Christ's body. Thank You for sending Your Son as our Redeemer, and for all things that remind us of His sacrifice. We remember Him in this act.

Vine:

Father, we give thanks for this fruit of the vine, representative of the blood that Jesus shed on the cross to gain victory for us over sin and death.

✝

John V. Richardson

Communion Prayer

Memories.... Memories.... Memories. We each have memories, precious memories. Some of you may remember a preacher we had years ago who was very big on memories of his grandfather's farm. Now I too have a farm and I sometimes bore you with memories of my childhood there. You are kind to me, and you listen. Well, I'm not the story teller that Marlin Connelly is, so I won't tell about those memories this morning.

Jesus told us how He wants to be remembered. He told us, through Scripture, many things we are to remember. He told us through example, that we should break bread and drink the cup in His memory ""until I come again," He said. The bread to remind us of His earthly body, the cup to remind us of the blood He shed for our sins.

Remember with me as we do both this morning.

Bread:

Thank you, Lord God, for this bread that is a representation of Your body, crucified on the Cross for us. Bless it, and bless us as we eat of it.

Wine:

Father God, bless this cup that represents to us Your blood, shed for our sins. Help us to remember His sacrifice.

Collection:

We do have precious memories of how Jesus has saved us. We have purposed in our hearts toward the work we intend at this place. And we anticipate that we will make sacrifices to meet this challenge. Let us give ever more generously to accomplish our goals.

Bless us, Holy Father, and lead us in sacrificial giving in the months to come. Your blessings, we remember, are countless. You have placed us in the richest nation on earth, with greater freedom than man has ever known. Most of all, You sacrificed Your own son for our salvation. We can never repay you. Help us to remember these blessings, and to witness to Your work in our lives, by building a useful facility in this community, through our own sacrificial giving.

✟

Vignettes

On September 11, 2002, the Alum Creek Church held a special memorial service. Orange Township Firemen were honored guests. One of the prayers was made by John Richardson.

Gracious and Compassionate Father:

Recently, we have been made acutely aware that everything we have and are comes from You. Every breath we take is by Your grace. Thank You, Father, for each and every blessing.

For this moment in time, we are stopped to remember and honor the fallen heroes who acted so unselfishly last year and gave their lives so that others might live. Jesus told us "Greater love has no one than this, that he lay down his life for his friends." The firemen in doing their duty at the World Trade Center, the passengers on Flight 93, and those at the Pentagon have become heroes to us all.

We honor their memory. Through those memories, they will live long into the future. Their heroics will be passed down from generation to generation. Our children and grandchildren will hear of their great deeds.

God, You gave Your only Son, Jesus, so that each of us could have life everlasting. These men and women gave their lives so that others could live. This nation will be forever grateful.

We pray for the families of all those who made this sacrifice, just as we pray for the families of those they were unable to reach. Give them peace as they deal with their loss.

Tonight we pray for the firemen of Orange Township, who stand ready to give their lives if need be. Be with them as they go about their duties. Protect their families. May they never face a disaster so tragic as did those who were in the Twin Towers.

Father, we are thankful for the United States of America, the country in which we live. Bless us and bless our leaders with wisdom. Make us into the peaceful nation that we profess to be. Help us to do only good in our world, to forgive our enemies, and to help mankind of whatever nation.

Through Jesus Christ, our Savior. And the whole church says: Amen.

✞

John V. Richardson

He Arose! He Arose!

Driving along the beautiful Muskingum River earlier this month, we saw a hand painted sign: **He is Risen.** I thought to myself, "Amen and Amen." The Good News of Jesus is spreading.

On the drive back into Columbus, we saw many signs of the approaching Easter celebration.

Then on a card from our family in Los Angeles, we read - "This is:

A Time to Reflect
A Time to Pray
A Time to Rejoice

And to each of these I say, "Amen."

Today, people throughout the world are assembling to celebrate Easter. My prayer is that we will remember the real reason we are assembled, today and every Sunday, is to worship that Risen Jesus!

Bread:

Lord, bless this bread as we break it together in the memory of the Risen Jesus, our brother and Savior.

Vine:

Thank you, God and Father, that we drink this cup in memory of Jesus ... He who died, was buried, and rose again ... for us and our sins.

Collection:

Father, God, thank You for all of our blessings. We realize that everything we have here on earth and in eternity is a gift from You.

May we give back joyfully of what we have to Your glory and to the work here at Alum Creek.

✢

Vignettes

Oklahoma Bombing

Recently, a memorial service was held for the 168 people killed in the bombing of the Federal Building in Oklahoma City. There was a period of silence to remember those people. There is a memorial building so that we can realize the proportions of the damage done and how these people died. These things were done so that we will remember the lives lost. We do need to remember our history.

Through the Scriptures, Jesus told us how we are to remember Him. He lifted the bread and broke it for His disciples, saying "Eat .... This is my body. Then He raised the cup and blessed it, saying "Drink of it for this is my blood of the covenant, poured out for the forgiveness of sin." Yes, Jesus died for our sins. Let us remember Him in this memorial.

Bread:

Father, bless this bread and each of us as we break it together with fellow believers throughout the world. Cause us to remember Jesus as we do so, considering His suffering upon the cross.

We rejoice that He arose from that death and ascended into heaven.

Fruit of the Vine:

Father, bless this cup and each of us as we drink it together. Help us to remember that Jesus died for our sins, not for His own, and that He ascended into heaven and is preparing a place for us there if we will but believe and obey.

Offering:

"Now concerning the collection for the saints, as I have given orders to the churches of the Galatians, so do you also. On the first day of the week, let each one of you lay something aside, storing up as he may prosper...."

For us just now, that is so that when the Building Contractor holds out his hand for that first check, our treasurer can write it and we'll all say "Thank You, God, for we do have it."

God, Heavenly Father, Father of us all:

Just as our earthly fathers provided for us when we were physically children, so You, Father, provide us with every need. We love and thank You!

✝

John V. Richardson

Two Cups

You remember, of course, that Jesus had sent Peter and John ahead to make preparation for the Passover Feast that they would share in Jerusalem. Luke continues his account:

"When the hour came, Jesus and his apostles reclined at the table .... Taking the cup, He gave thanks and said 'Take this and divide it among you . For I tell you I will not drink again of the fruit of the vine until the kingdom of God comes.'"

Unless we understand their customs, we are puzzled by the two cups, for, after the meal, Jesus again takes up the cup. The first cup is a part of Passover meals even today. It is the Cup of Blessing, taken in awareness of what God had done for them. He had delivered them out of Egypt and now they could recline at the table - Before, they had to stand and serve their Egyptian masters.

Luke continues with the verses we know so well: "And He took bread, gave thanks, and broke it, and gave it to them, saying, 'This is my body given for you; do this in remembrance of Me.' In the same way, after the supper He took the cup, saying 'This cup is the new covenant in my blood, which is poured out for you.'"

The Jews, while they still observe Passover and take that first cup, the Cup of Blessing, have no part in our observance of the New Covenant, since they have not claimed this greatest of blessing. This morning, we remember not the Passover (although it is a part of the heritage we claim) but we remember the perfect sacrifice that our Lord made for our sins. Pray with me while we remember.

Bread:

Thank You, Lord, for this bread, this symbol of your broken body. Bless us as we break bread together.

Cup:

Thank You, Lord, for this cup, this symbol of Your shed blood, given for our sins which You remember no more. Bless it and us as we drink it together.

✝

Vignettes

Memory

Memory is a beautiful thing. God knew what He was doing when He gave us the ability to remember.

Last Saturday, Hope and I were in Toledo for the wedding of the young woman we sometimes think of as being our daughter. During that ceremony, I remembered my own wedding, more than 58 years ago. It is a beautiful memory; Hope was a beautiful bride.

When the best man toasted the newly married couple, my mind drifted off to a Sunday evening Bible Class this spring. We were studying the miracles of Jesus. Don Davis read the passage about Jesus turning water into wine at a wedding feast and made the comment, "That would have been a lot of wine!" Which prompted me to calculate just how much it might have been:
6 stone jars
20-30 gallons each, say 25, average - that's 150 gallons

Our glasses last Saturday held about 4 oz. each, about 4800 gallons at Jesus' wedding feast, or 2400 guests could have had two glasses each. Like Don said, "That's a lot of wine!" - or a very big wedding!!

Yes, God knew what He was doing when He gave us the gift of remembering. Ruth Morrow - or someone else, this morning - remembered to fill the trays before worship this morning. The Apostle Paul told the Corinthians (and us) to remember how Jesus took the bread and commanded us to eat. He asks us to remember Jesus' words: "This is my body which is given for you. Do this in remembrance of me."

So we, the church, the Bride of Christ, come to that Wedding Feast this morning.

Bread:

Bless this bread, and us, Lord. Help us to remember the teachings of Jesus, to remember all His great deeds, and especially His sacrifice for us.

Wine:

Bless this cup, and us, Lord. Prompt us to remember this New Covenant, help us to proclaim Your death, until You come again.

✠

John V. Richardson

Take This Bread

Rick Cochran, husband of Hope's niece Melodee, was part of a group called Faithful Friends: he wrote music and sang with them. In 1993 they made a tape, "Living Waters." Rick gave a copy to John Richardson, who used it for a communion service.

"Take this bread," is what Jesus said. "It's a promise I'm making to you. If you believe There is more you'll receive Than on earth what is given to you."

He said, "Take it and eat it, as often as you do, Remember, my body's been given for you. Your sins are forgiven; I died to clean your soul. Receive my Spirit; your life will be whole.

Bread:

"Drink this wine, for the blood will be mine On the cross I'll be shedding for you. If you believe There is more you'll receive Then on earth what is given to you."

"He said, "Take it and drink it as oft as you do Remember the Blood of the Lamb shed for you. Your sins are forgiven. I died to clean your soul. Receive my Spirit; your life will be whole.

Wine:

"Rise from this table; rise and go in peace. My Spirit is with you, my love will never cease. Remember this promise I'm making to you. I'll be there if you need me, whatever you do."

He said, "Eat it and drink it, as oft as you do, Remember this promise I'm making to you.

✟

Vignettes

3. Wedding Prayers

On June 21, 1980, Mike and Marlyis Zelnik were married at Indian Springs. John was asked to bless them and their new life together.

Zelnik Wedding

O Lord God and our Creator,

The One Who loves us all:

Your plan for us and for our lives is loving and right. We praise and thank You. In the beginning, You created us male and female. Therefore, today Michael leaves his father and mother and cleaves to Marlyis as they become one flesh. You have brought these two together to share life within Your plan. Bless them from this day forward until death do them part.

Help Mike and Marlyis each to be patient, understanding, humble, meek, and forgiving with the other. Bind their marriage in Your perfect love. Grant them faithfulness to each other and to You. You have given Christ to be their example and their Savior. Let others look at their life together and see that they do "love the Lord."

Give Mike special love and patience with his new sons. May Justin and Ean be loving and obedient children, obeying Your will.

Remind those of us who witness this marriage of our own commitment to pray for and support this new family in every way that we can.

Bless Michael and Marlyis now as they make their marriage vows to each other, before You, God, and in our witness.

✝

John V. Richardson

In 1997, when Lori Miller and Tom Ross wanted to be married, they decided to have two ceremonies. John Richardson was asked to do the religious wedding while a judge did the legal portion. The religious ceremony was at Indian Springs on Christmas Day Evening, while family members were in town; the legal part was done at Port Columbus, where the judge was catching a flight.

Ross Wedding Ceremony

We have gathered to hear Tom and Lori pledge themselves to each other in marriage.

Do you, Tom, take this woman to be your lawful wedded wife, to love and respect her, honor and cherish her, In health and in sickness, In prosperity and adversity,

and leaving all others, keep yourself only for her, so long as you both shall live? (Tom: "I do.")

Do you, Lori, in like manner, agree to receive Tom as your lawful wedded husband, to love and respect him, to live with him in all faith and tenderness, in health and in sickness, in prosperity and in adversity,

and leaving all others, keep yourself only for him, so long as you both shall live? (Lori: "I do.")

Rings are being exchanged; these precious circles serve as a token and pledge of the purity and never-ending love you share for your chosen companion in life.

Tom, place the ring on Lori's finger, and repeat after me: "This ring I give to you (Tom repeats) In token and in pledge (Tom repeats) Of our constant faith (Tom repeats) And abiding love." (Tom repeats)

Lori, place the ring on Tom's finger, and repeat after me: "This ring I give to you (Lori repeats) In token and in pledge (Lori repeats) Of our constant faith (Lori repeats) And abiding love." (Lori repeats)

Tom and Lori, you have agreed to enter the marriage relationship and have given and received rings in token and pledge of your love and faith. I now declare that you are husband and wife according to my authority as God's minister and by His ordinances.

✟

Vignettes

Prayer

Sovereign Lord, Lord of our lives, we have heard from Tom and Lori their acceptance of the solemn and significant vows of marriage. We pray You will grant them grace and courage, love and loyalty, constancy and faith, so that they will maintain their vows to the end of their lives.

May their home radiate the sunshine of Your love. May all who come into the circle be enriched and ennobled. May they ever witness to You and Your power.

We ask this through Christ, who shares in this sacred institution. Amen.

Just as Tom and Lori have pledged themselves to each other, I now ask us each, family or friend, to promise to uphold and support them in their new together. Answer by saying "I do."

✝

John V. Richardson

4. Prayers of Memorial

In November of 1996, Charlie O'Donnell of Prairie Village, Kansas, died. He loved Morgan County, birthplace of his wife, June; and they were longtime friends of the Richardson family. His widow June asked John to conduct a graveside service for him when he was buried in Zion Cemetery, Portersville, Ohio.

Graveside Service for O'Donnell

Ecclesiastes tells us, "For everything there is a season, a time for every matter under heaven. A time to be born and a time to die, a time to weep and a time to laugh."

We have gathered today to celebrate the life of Charles W. O'Donnell. Most of us have known Charlie for years. We have walked together with him through good times and bad, through laughter and tears.

Today, we can walk no further with Charlie; we must wait here while Charlie goes on to walk even more closely with God. True, God walks with us, as He did with Charlie, through all our lives here on earth. So, remember,

"Let not your hearts be troubled. Believe in God," Jesus said. And "Believe also in me. In my Father's house are many rooms. If it were not so, would I go to prepare a place for you?" And, "I will come again and will take you to myself, that where I am you may be also. You know the way where I am going."

Charlie has gone ahead of us to collect on that promise.

Goodbyes are so difficult. We all have problems with goodbyes, with grief. Yet grieving is a necessary part of our healing. We must realize that death is only a continuation of life. There is a time for everything and this is the moment of our parting. We will grieve, and we will heal. As we say this final goodbye, let us pray:

Heavenly Father, As we commit the earthly remains of Charlie O'Donnell to the earth again, we pray for the healing of our hearts. Thank you that he was a part of our lives for a time.

Comfort his wife, June, in her loss.

Comfort his son, Pat, in his loss.

Comfort Maria, who has been his daughter,

Comfort the dear grandchildren - Laura and Carmen and John.

Comfort us all, relatives and friends, who mourn Charlie today.

Thank you for hearing and answering our prayer.

In the name of Christ Jesus, our Savior.

✝

Vignettes

Stewart Memorial

Heavenly Father:

We come to You praising Your name, recognizing You as our Creator. You bring us into this world that You created for us. You know our every thought. You know our every need and You know our prayer even before we utter it.

You are Magnificent.

You "so loved the world that You gave Your only Son that who so ever believes in Him should not perish but have eternal life."

Larry Stewart searched for and found You, source of eternal life. Larry came to know Your son Jesus as the bread of life. Larry ate of this bread. He will live forever. We are thankful.

We hardly knew Larry and his years were short. But he touched our lives and your body here at Indian Springs. Through him, we know and serve his family. Larry was our brother. We thank You for his earthly life, and we leave him safe in Your arms.

Our petition today is for those of us who mourn Larry's passing. Give us his faith and understanding of You, our Lord God. We ask peace for his family in the coming days. Lift up their spirits, remove all pain from their aching hearts, and give them Your peace and Your love.

✝

John V. Richardson

Psalm 121 was Evelyn Gordon's favorite. Hope Richardson read it to her repeatedly during the days of her final illness. Evelyn was reminded by it of the hills of Morgan County. John read it during her graveside service for the family.

Prayer for Gordon

Our Loving Father, Creator, God:

We lift up to You the spirit of our sister Evelyn Gordon.

Father, each of us - relative or friend - will cherish forever the memory of Evelyn. She loved You, Lord, she loved her church, she loved her family, she loved her friends. She had a beautiful Christian relationship with all with whom she came in contact. She touched our lives in so many ways.

Oh, Father, we will miss her presence with us. Evelyn had such a deep love for Your creation, Father. She saw and heard the things in nature which others of us rarely see or hear. She had a discerning ear as she listened to the birdsong in trees and meadow. Her keen eyes missed little as she walked through Your pastures and woodlands.

Father, wipe away the tears from our eyes this morning. Wipe the tears of sorrow from the eyes of loved ones, relatives and friends, as we grieve together. Replace those tears of grief with tears of gladness and rejoicing: Evelyn has been released from the pain and suffering and cares of this world; let us only rejoice that she is safe with You at last.

Father, may we each share a little of her great faith and belief in You, our Creator, and in Jesus Christ, our Redeemer.

We commend her spirit to Your safe keeping until we, too, cross the bridge from this world to eternity with You.

In Jesus' name, Amen.

✟

Vignettes

In 1981, Leonard Rucker, a retired preacher whom Indian Springs had helped to support for several years, died at the age of 82. A memorial service was held and John Richardson was assigned one of the prayers.

Prayer for Leonard Rucker

Almighty God... Father of Mankind... Creator of the Earth and all therein... Ruler of the Universe...

We honor Your holy name.

Your power is displayed throughout all creation, but nowhere so much as in the resurrection of Your Son. Together with Leonard Rucker, we look forward to our own resurrection.

Truly, we are more than conquerors through You. Nothing can separate us from Your love - neither death nor life nor angels nor principalities nor things present nor height nor depth nor anything else in all creation can separate us from you. You love us; let us never outlive our love for you.

Be with us as we pick up our everyday lives without our brother Leonard. Help us to be the witness for You and Your power that Leonard was.

In Christ Jesus Our Lord we do pray.

☦

5. *Specific Prayers*

In early 2000, Lynn Harris was diagnosed as having breast cancer. Hope ordered pink ribbons, and these were distributed to the congregation. Lynn was called forward so that she could stand with John while he worded a special prayer.

Prayer for Healing

We give thanks to You, our God and our Savior. We call upon Your name and remember Your wondrous acts of healing. We know that you hear our prayers and answer them. We know that You are aware of our needs before we even express them.

Father, today we lift up to You our sister Lynn Harris and her family, Val and the children, Beth and Tim. You have already answered our prayer when Lynn was diagnosed as having lobular carcinoma and not cancer. We each know something of the agony connected with human diseases.

We pray for the Harris's that they will feel confidence and peace in dealing with this situation. Relieve the tensions connected with their decision-making, with the waiting for lab results and for doctor's reports. Strengthen their faith and grant them peace of mind.

Guide each of us to be concerned and helpful.

And God we pray for a cure for the dreaded disease of breast cancer will be found, so that our women need not be concerned.

Thank you, God, for hearing us...

Thank you, God, for answering our prayers.

✝

Vignettes

Paul and Barbara Young's family were close friends during the Indian Springs days. John, as an Elder, baptized Lisa, the eldest daughter, and made special prayers on several occasions.

O Lord, Our God and Our Creator: Hallowed be Thy name.

Tonight we rejoice and celebrate with Lisa Young and with her parents in Lisa's accomplishment. She has met the requirements set down by our university, Ohio State, and has been granted her degree. Now she is about to step into her adult life.

Father, we praise You for Lisa's belief in and trust in You. We praise You for her life and witness.

Tonight our prayer is special for Lisa ... may she ever walk blameless in Your sight, doing that which is right. May Lisa ever speak truth from her heart, as she has been taught by loving parents and grandparents [Lisa's grandparents were the preacher, Brother Traylor and his wife].

We pray that Lisa will never slander with her tongue, that she will ever witness for You, and praise You.

May Lisa never do evil nor bring reproach to Your name. May her friends be scattered over all the earth, wherever your children are found.

May Lisa ever sojourn in Thy tent and may she dwell on Thy holy hill.

✟

Dear Lord, our Father:

Thank You that we can be present to celebrate this happy occasion with Bret Young and his family. You have blessed Bret with a keen and inquisitive mind and we are thankful for this. We are thankful for having known Bret and for the influence he has had on each of our lives. No one can "despise him for his youth. We love and respect him as our brother.

As Bret goes on to college and into the walk of life for which you have chosen him, we pray that he will continue to set an example to all whom he meets - in speech, in conduct, in love, in faith and purity. We pray that Bret will turn to You in his happy times and in his times of trial. Keep him always faithful and obedient to you, Father.

And now we thank You for the food prepared in celebration of this day. Bless the love manifest through it, and the fellowship of our joining together in it. Let us each always serve You with the strength You grant to us.

✟

John V. Richardson

Dear Father, God, Creator:

We come to You with thanksgiving and praise in our hearts. We praise You because You have created both the heavens and the earth. In the beginning, Your Spirit moved over the face of the waters. You said "Let there be light" and there was light. You created all living things of the land and sea and air. When all things were ready, You created us, Your children. None other is as powerful or majestic as You. We praise You as the light of the world.

It is to You that we come in prayer, lifting up to You, Sara Both Young, one of Your children from Your creation. We come in thanksgiving for her decision to give her life to You through Jesus Christ, her Savior. We know You accept her into Your loving arms as one of Yours. Protect her and guide her all the days of her life, wherever You lead her.

We are thankful for all those who have witnessed of You to her and we are thankful so many of us are here with her this morning.

We know that we are justified by faith and we have peace with You, God, through our Lord Jesus Christ. May Sara Beth's faith continue to grow and never falter. May your peace be her peace. It is in the name of Your son, Jesus Christ, that we approach Your throne.

Amen.

We love you, Sara Beth! [Prayer was given at the time of her baptism on June 29, 1980 by J. Russell Corley].

✟

Vignettes

Barbara Kay Corley

In early 1980, a baby girl named Barbara Kay was born to Russ and Gena Corley. A few weeks later, they asked to have her dedicated to God before the congregation at Indian Springs. John Richardson was pleased to oblige, and used this format:

"This is a significant moment in the lives of the Corleys. We are here to give thanks to God for the precious gift of life which He has placed in their care. Russ and Gena, will you please stand.

Do you, Russ, and you, Gena, take this child, Barbara Kay, to rear in the sight of our Lord? Will you guide her through all of your lives, using Christ Jesus as your example? (Answer: We do.)

Blessed be the name of the Lord!

As the extended family of the Corleys, we of Indian Springs will also love and care for Barbara Kay. Some of us will be her Bible teachers, all of us will serve as examples to her. Do we accept this charge? (Answer: We do.)

Blessed be the name of the Lord!

Prayer

O Lord our God, Creator of each of us: We praise Thee for Thou art fearful and wonderful. Wonderful are Thy works. You know our inward parts. You know us well, for You did knit us together in our mother's womb.

We stand before You today in a spirit of thanksgiving and celebration because of this child, Barbara Kay Corley. We know of the yearning in the hearts of these young parents for this child. We know of their joy in her safe and healthy arrival. Thank You for granting her to them.

Father, we ask for Gena and Russ that You continue to give them a strong love for each other and for Barbara Kay. We pray that they will nurture her in Your ways, teaching her "indoors and out of doors, when they lie down, and when they rise." Give Russ and

John V. Richardson

Gena understanding and gentleness and patience with this new soul. She is a gift from You.

For all those of us of Indian Springs, we pray that we will never shirk our portion of the rearing of this child. Let us be Christ like examples for her to follow.

We pray that as Barbara Kay grows in stature, she will grow in wisdom and in favor with You and with her fellow man, that she will dedicate her life to serving You, our Lord. Bestow a double portion of Thy Spirit on her. Give her a life blessed with grace and peace and love. Let her resist temptations and overcome evils. Bless her on earth and in heaven. Yea, we pray that at the end of a life lived for You, Barbara Kay -- and her parents, Russ and Gena, yea even each soul of us, may hear: "Well done, thou good and faithful servant; enter into the joys of Thy Lord."

Because of Christ and His love for us, Amen.

✝

A Prayer for Kay

In the year 2002, Hope's sister Kay was diagnosed with colon cancer. After surgery, she was subjected to months of chemotherapy. She was given such strength that she was able to work daily, not using any sick leave, and was pronounced free of cancer at the end of that time. John prayed for her, at her request.

Prayer

Our Father in Heaven: Hallowed by Thy name.

We praise Your name. We thank You for Your love and concern for us. We come knowing that You hear our prayers, and that You answer us.

Father, we lift Kay up to You. She loves and serves You. We thank You for her, for the life You have given to her. The beauty You have given to her. The husband and daughter and granddaughter You have given to her. As You have commanded, she loves and serves others. She is wife, mother, grandmother, servant to us all, helping so many in so many ways. Bless her, Father.

While Kay waits for the results of the biopsy, relieve her anxiety and still her racing heart and mind. Give her Your "peace that passeth understanding," and may she have a restful night tonight.

We pray, Father, for a good report tomorrow. Strengthen her faith, help her not to be discouraged, to keep a positive attitude, to remember that You have promised "All things work together for the good of those who love You."

Forgive us for our doubting, accept and answer our fervent prayers. We love Kay. Heal her.

In Jesus' name. Amen.

✟

John V. Richardson

Appendix 6. A Day with the Post Engineer

"A Day with the Post Engineer"
By Hugo Spagaldiochi
Possible pseudonym of Private Gordon C. Newell,
Company Clerk to Lieutenant John V. Richardson,
Post Engineer of the 182nd General Hospital aka Sudbury Park Hospital

Written circa 1944

It was a beautiful English morning when the Post Engineer tore himself from the confines of his feather bed. By the time our stalwart hero had donned his motley coveralls the beautiful English morning had ceased to exist and it was now <u>pouring</u> down rain. His heart said that it would be a fine day for a day off but his sense of duty, so well built up in his twelve years of army life, forced him out into the downpour.

As he struggled through the proponderous [sic] seas of mud his thoughts returned to Ohio and the drought that they must be having, but again his sense of duty pushed him beyond the endurance of the human body. As he entered the Officers Club for breakfast, he noticed that everyone else had taken the day off. This made him a bit discouraged and he didn't have much appetite for his hardtack and powdered eggs. After a few plates of powdered eggs, his old engineer fighting spirit returned to him and gave e him the intestinal fortitude to look forward to the day's work with great anxiety.

Gathering his staff around him he issued his orders of the day. First on the list was three miles or pavement around the area so that the Colonel could ride a jeep on inspection tours instead or the usual walking. The second man drew the job of constructing three prefabricated buildings complete with windows and stoves. Ten men were dispatched to the mess hall for the mess officers fancy. One man followed an absent-minded Major around to mark down the changes in his mind. The plumbers were sent down to the surgical side where the drains were more than likely clogged, the rest were dispatched to harass the British. The electrician was asleep.

That accomplished the Post Engineer picked up the morning Gazette to catch up on the news of the hard working troops at the front. Five minutes later we find our hero busily talking into three telephones. In one he was saying "Yes sir" to the Colonel who wanted a priority job done on the building of four brick wards where there was now a forest; he figured 36 hours was enough on that. The second phone was a direct wire to the utilities sergeant who kept a staff of four secretaries writing down the work that poured in through the third phone.

At this time a cockney driver brought in the daily truck load of work requests. The clerk was now asleep. The driver offered the Post Engineer an American cigarette and warmed his hind quarters by the stove before venturing out in the rain again.
Thus the morning passed. At twelve the Post Engineer took his shots of adrenalin and morphine and set out for lunch at the club.

On approaching the fire house one would never suspect that this quiet little place was the scene of many battles as fierce as the most bloody battles on the front. It was, for a fact, generally quiet within the office of the Post Engineer, but it is not of those times that we wish to speak for the topic of the little sketch concerns itself with the moments that have become almost too prevalent in the last few weeks.

Upon entering the office, one would get the idea that it was the center for a very thriving organization, but on closer inspection you would notice that the Post Engineer was not busily looking up facts in the latest field manual but was instead reading the latest issue of the Manchester Gazette. The clerk on closer inspection was found to be typing letters home with the pretense of typing letters of very secret nature to the District Commander of the Royal Engineers.

When the fateful hour of eleven was reached the office ceased to be a center of malingering and became the battlefield that I have mentioned before. The signal for hostilities was the kick of the Engineer's foot as he bluntly aroused his clerk. The clerk sensing the situation in the moment grabbed a folder that he kept ever present for such occasions. The Leftenant [sic] being ambidextrous took the folder in one hand and the telephone in the other. After exchanging the time of day with one of the cute telephone operators (the Leftenant's wife of course suspects nothing), and politely asked for the office of the DCRE.

In the moment that he was forced to wait for his connection, the Post Engineer ran his feet through a box of broken glass so that he would get in an appropriate mood. "Office of the District Commander of the Royal Engineers-- Major Alphonse Mercum Robertson District Commander of the Royal Engineers speaking," came from the other end of the line.

"Major, this is the Post Engineer for the Sudbury Park Hospital and upon checking my records, I find that I ordered one dozen roofing nails two years ago and I was wondering if you had gotten those in yet?" "Well, said the Major, "I will look in my records and see what has happened to them. The leftenant then heard a muffled oath from the Major and a loud call to his assistant to look in the trash pile for the aforementioned order. A few hours later, the Major came back with, "Why yes, leftenant I find that order and we ordered them from Derby and we expect them sometime this year." The leftenant, who was by this time a bright shade of purple, was about to lose control of himself when he again heard the Major's sweet voice. "Let me read you a directive that came out only yesterday that is vitally connected with your order, it reads as follows: The extreme shortage of tungsten in this country has forced us to make all lamp filaments out of iron and therefore they cannot be expected to last as long as the old type of filaments. The supply of the lamps is no greater now than before so it is essential that extreme care be used in the use of light bulbs. Of course leftenant since light bulbs are not an Engineer supply. Getting back to the nails it is our usual procedure to send out a tracer on goods not delivered in five years so if the nails don't come through in the next two years we will automatically send out a tracer. Goodbye Leftenant."

The Post Engineer could not answer, for at this time the attendants where helping him into his straight jacket and were hustling him to the psychopathic ward for a short rest.

With this we will close another chapter in the life of the Post Engineer and will leave the clerk to his letter writing, as our hero recuperates from the battle.

* * *

Whistling merrily our gallant knight entered his office ready to accomplish the impossible. He was greeted by twenty odd looking chariters (sic) that were carrying on a conversation in a heavy accent. This was the clerk of works and his gang of yes men. The clerk of works muttered a greeting while stroking his mustache and informed the chief that he could only get three jills of paint instead of the promised twenty gallons. The mob then stepped out for tea.

At this point the lights flickered and went out. Like a streak of lightning, our hero was out in the area climbing poles peering into fuse boxes, and generally trying to find out where the British had put all the wires. He was closely followed by a queer looking gentleman who said over and over, "But, I tell you Lieutenant you can't have the current off right now." We learned later that this was the head of X-Ray.

By this time the British electrician had joined our electrician in bed. The clerk was asleep.

The lights fixed, the PE dragged himself back to the office for a shot of fruit cocktail only to find a Nurse frantically demanding five gallons of lavender paint for, her commode seats. She was gently dropped through the floor into a pit of hungry lions.

"Have YOU seen my grass cutting tools?" said a voice from the door. By this time, the Colonel had changed his mind and wanted the wards built in a swamp on the other side or camp. Hurriedly explaining the change to his men, he went to dress for retreat because as a side line he was also a detachment commander. As he went out the door, he saw the electrician preparing to go to town. The clerk was reading now.

After dinner, the post engineer spray painted three mess halls for the Colonel who thought they would look better in cream.

This he accomplished by five thirty, so he fought his way through the blinding storm to his billet where he hoped that he could get an hour and a half of good sleep.

With this we will leave our hero, the Post Engineer, in the passionate arms of Morpheus preparing for another day.

Lightly edited: for format, mostly spelling errors, and punctuation, by Dr. John V. Richardson Jr., UCLA.

John V. Richardson

COLOPHON

Started: 4 December 1994; continued: 6 December 1995
Initial Microsoft Word Input: Winter 1996 and Spring 1997
Father's Revisions: 12 May 1997
Minor Green Line Changes: 13 May 1997
Omnipage Pro 8.0 scan using HP ScanJet 4c: 29 December 1998
Omnipage Pro 9.0 Rescan: 30 December 1998
Edit Scan: 4 January 1999

Corrections and Additions: 29 June 1999
Additions: 9 August 2000; 18 and 24 July 2001; 22 April 2002;
21 December 2002; 27 July 2004; and 28 December 2004;
29 April 2006; 20-24 July 2007; 19-20 February 2009
And 10 and 13 April 2009
Photographs added: 7 April 2007, 4 March 2009, and 13 April 2009

Penultimate Revisions: 14-15, 20 April 2009; 12 May 2009;
23 June 2009; 11 July 2009, 4 and 7 August 2009, 14 September 2009, 15
December 2009
5 January 2010; and 20 April 2012;
Appendix 6 added: 11 May 2012

More formatting: 31 August 2013
Final edits: 7 and 9 September 2013

www.ingramcontent.com/pod-product-compliance
Lightning Source LLC
Chambersburg PA
CBHW021240090426
42740CB00006B/626